HEALING AFTER
JOB LOSS

Also by Alan Wolfelt:

Creating Meaningful Funeral Ceremonies:
A Guide for Families

Healing a Child's Grieving Heart:
100 Practical Ideas for Families,
Friends and Caregivers

Healing a Friend's Grieving Heart:
100 Practical Ideas for Helping Someone
You Love Through Loss

Healing Your Grieving Heart for Kids:
100 Practical Ideas

The Journey Through Grief:
Reflections on Healing

Understanding Your Grief:
Ten Essential Touchstones for Finding
Hope and Healing Your Heart

The Wilderness of Grief: Finding Your Way

Companion Press is dedicated to the education and support of both the bereaved and bereavement caregivers. We believe that those who companion the bereaved by walking with them as they journey in grief have a wondrous opportunity: to help others embrace and grow through grief—and to lead fuller, more deeply-lived lives themselves because of this important ministry.

Companion
P R E S S

For a complete catalog and ordering information, write or call:

Companion Press
The Center for Loss and Life Transition
3735 Broken Bow Road
Fort Collins, CO 80526
(970) 226-6050
www.centerforloss.com

HEALING
AFTER JOB LOSS

·

100 PRACTICAL IDEAS

TIPS AND ACTIVITIES TO HELP YOU
UNDERSTAND AND TRANSCEND YOUR
GRIEF AFTER THE LOSS OF A JOB

·

ALAN D. WOLFELT, PH.D.

Companion
P R E S S

Fort Collins, Colorado
An imprint of the Center for Loss and Life Transition

Companion Press is an imprint of the
Center for Loss and Life Transition,
3735 Broken Bow Road, Fort Collins, Colorado 80526
970-226-6050
www.centerforloss.com

Companion Press books may be purchased in bulk for sales promotions, premiums or fundraisers. Please contact the publisher at the above address for more information.

Printed in the United States of America

14 13 12 11 10   5 4 3 2 1

ISBN: 978-1-879651-69-2

INTRODUCTION

Across the world, people have fallen on hard times. The worldwide recession has created tough marketplaces where the language of cuts, closures, downsizing, and conservation dominate the talk of workplace leaders. In the United States, 14.8 million people are unemployed as of September 2010, according to the US Bureau of Labor Statistics. Millions more have been affected by salary cuts, underemployment, furloughs, and change to part-time status. Employees at all levels have been affected—from frontline workers to executives, and everyone in between.

Maybe you are one of them.

It may bring you little comfort to know you are not alone. After all, job loss is personal. It is you who has had her daily routine turned upside-down. It is you who has had his ability to make money stripped away from him.

While finding a new job is undoubtedly at the top of your to-do list, consider this: In order to be job-ready, you must first acknowledge and work through your natural feelings of loss. With job loss, it's normal to feel angry, anxious, unsure, and even depressed. These feelings can permeate not only your day but your motivation and self-confidence. And if they are not healed, they can ultimately affect your search for a new job and your long-term happiness.

Job loss is a major life loss that demands attention and care. Often, our identities are tied up in what we do for a living. When we first meet someone, one of the first questions asked is, "What do you do?" You must now work through the difficult but necessary process of redefining yourself. But always keep in mind: what you did for work is only one dimension of who you are as a person, and work is only one aspect of your life.

Be patient and practice self-compassion

You've just been knocked down when you weren't looking. Even the terms used to describe job losses—right-sized, pruned-out, and downsized—may provoke feelings of rejection, resignation, and hopelessness. Yet down is not where you have to stay.

Yes, you need a new job. Yes, you need to earn money. But no matter how much you want these things, they will take time. On average, Americans spend about four to seven months searching for a new job after losing one—and this process can take much longer for certain kinds of jobs, especially during this recession. You might feel like you have to put all other aspects of your life on hold and that if you don't spend every minute of the day searching, you're not trying hard enough.

Go easy on yourself. Set worry aside and take a deep breath. We've got a plan that will help.

The five central needs of healing after job loss

As a grief counselor and the Director of the Center for Loss and Life Transition in Colorado, I, Dr. Alan Wolfelt, have made it my life's work to help people with grief and mourning, including job loss. This book's co-author, Dr. Kirby Duvall, is a board-certified family practice physician with years of experience counseling people on loss and transition at his practice, which is based in the offices of a global manufacturing company.

In this book, we give you 100 practical ideas to help you move from the reality of your loss to mourning and reconciling that loss. We then encourage you through simple practices to set your intention, take action, and allow for transformation into your next job or career. We've divided the 100 practical ideas under five central needs of healing after job loss:

1. The first central need, *Acknowledge the Reality of Your Loss*, helps you take a fresh look at your job loss and inventory your many thoughts and feelings.
2. Need two, *Allow Yourself to Mourn*, encourages you to recognize your grief during this naturally difficult time and supports you to mourn—to process your grief about your job loss.
3. Central need three, *Set Your Intention*, helps you get mentally, emotionally, and spiritually ready for your future work and life.
4. Need four, *Take Action*, provides specific strategies to turn your intent into action.
5. Finally, need five, *Allow for Transformation*, supports you in embracing the changes that come with a new job and finding meaning and purpose in your new work life.

How to use this book

Someone very wise once observed, "Every day, every moment, every second, there is a choice." Right this moment you have a choice. You can sit back, wait, and worry. Or you can read this practical resource, take action, and regain your ability to make a living and find job satisfaction. We hope to inspire you to be proactive and set in motion today the plans that will serve you well tomorrow.

This book is designed to help you get back into the job market. We will remind you that your future work life depends not so much on what has happened to you, but on how you cope with it. We will inspire you to acknowledge your job loss, yet urge you to turn your hope—your *expectations of the good that is yet to be*—toward the future.

Your future job security is in many ways the result of strategic planning, flexibility, and exploring your options. These we'll do as we journey through the central needs of healing together. Yet, your future job prospects are also anchored in your attitude. By applying these practical ideas, you'll clean house, if you will, after your job loss and go forward with a positive, open attitude. A good attitude allows you to actively create new opportunities for yourself and invent your own unique work future. No employer can provide you with this kind of security.

By completing the 100 ideas in this book, you'll create self-security by ridding yourself of unhelpful assumptions you may have made—assumptions about why you lost your job and your prospects for the future. Instead, you'll be left with ample ideas to move forward, feel encouraged, and make a plan for your job future.

These 100 ideas are practical, here-and-now, action-oriented tips. Each idea includes a brief explanation of a healing or inspiring concept followed by practical ways to apply the concept. On the bottom of each page, you'll notice a Carpe Diem section. As fans of the movie *Dead Poet's Society* will remember, *carpe diem* means *seize the day*. The intent of these tips is to give you something you can do in mere minutes to keep you moving toward healing and reconstructing your career. If nothing else, doing these every day will help you keep your momentum.

Don't relegate this book to your shelves. Keep it handy on your nightstand or desk. Better yet, carry it with you. Pick it up for some quick inspiration or ideas on carrying out your action plan. And, as the well-known saying goes, "Take what you can use and leave the rest." If you come to an idea that doesn't seem to fit, simply ignore it and flip to another page.

Job loss can be a grim, dark place that harbors feelings of failure and confusion. It's like suddenly being relegated to the basement after experiencing the sunny first floor. Think of these tips as steps toward an imaginary glass door. The more steps you take, the brighter the light gets. Soon enough, you'll be standing in front of that door, ready to turn the handle and walk through to your new future.

We are honored to take this journey of healing your job loss and moving toward a brighter future with you. Carpe diem!

CENTRAL NEED OF HEALING 1:

ACKNOWLEDGE THE REALITY OF YOUR JOB LOSS

Losing a job has understandably sent you into shock and disbelief. At first, you'll simply reel. You'll ask a lot of questions about why it happened. You'll have a lot of emotions and thoughts racing around in your head. You'll grieve your job loss. Be gentle with yourself. Now is the time to take care of your body, find comfort, and accept support from family and friends. In time, and after the shock dissipates, you will come to grips with the reality of your loss and move beyond it into a life that's transformed—for the better.

1.

RECOGNIZE JOB LOSS AS A LOSS

- You've lost your job. That's a big deal. The loss of a job is a major life loss because something that you truly valued is no longer a part of your life.

- Most likely, even if you weren't crazy about your job, there were things about it that you valued. Now these aspects are gone. Maybe you miss the:
  - Challenges of your work
  - Coworkers
  - Comfort of your daily routine
  - Energy in your work environment
  - Creativity that you expressed through your work
  - Security of income, retirement plans, and health insurance
  - Identity and self-worth offered by your position

- Just as when you lose someone you love to death or divorce, you feel the loss of your job—maybe not to the same extent, but the loss is palpable and real. It shakes up your life and self-confidence.

- Job loss creates strong emotions. At first, you may feel devastated and shocked. These feelings might turn to anger, sadness, or self-doubt. Maybe you feel a sense of emptiness or even anger at the injustice of being let go, or at how it was carried out. You could be having racing thoughts about what you should do next. All these feelings are normal after a job loss.

CARPE DIEM

Consider what you valued most about your job. Was it the break-room conversations, the feeling of being in charge, or the mental challenge of carrying out your duties? Find practical ways to soften a particular loss, today. For example, if you miss coworkers, call your favorites and set up a lunch or coffee date. If it was the challenge, pick up an old project and consider starting it up again.

2.

REALIZE THAT YOU LOST MORE THAN YOUR JOB

- Yes, you've lost your job, but you've also lost all the little things that go with it. Not only have you lost your source of income, you may have also lost your sense of economic stability, security, and a feeling that you have control over your life.

- Along with the loss of your job title and position, you may have lost some of your self-identity and self worth. Maybe you don't see yourself in as positive a light as you did before. Your certainty in your career and job path—and thus your sense of self—has been shaken.

- You may also have lost a feeling that you held status or rank in the community. You may feel disconnected and no longer involved.

- Each of these items demonstrates individual losses that you have endured. Add them up and you've taken a big hit. Honor the impact of this loss. You have been through a lot, and you need to be gentle with yourself and allow yourself to grieve and mourn before moving forward.

CARPE DIEM

Make a quick list of all the losses, big and small, that you've experienced during this job loss. Honor each one as having an impact on how you are currently feeling.

3.

UNDERSTAND GRIEF AS
A PART OF JOB LOSS

- When we think of grieving, we usually associate it with a death of someone we love. Yet grief is a part of every significant loss that we encounter in our lives—including job loss.

- We grieve when we lose something that we value. With grief comes a wide range of emotions. Commonly, people who are in grief experience shock and numbness, confusion, anxiety, guilt, regret, and even anger, blame, resentment, sadness, and sometimes relief. All these feelings can be overwhelming.

- In the early days after the job loss, your pain may seem ever-present. Seek refuge. It's okay to escape for a few hours every day and take a break from your feelings. You could:

  - Go for a walk
  - Read a book
  - Watch a movie
  - Join an online social network
  - Have coffee with a supportive friend
  - Spend time with your family

CARPE DIEM

Do something that brings you comfort. Maybe it's baking an apple pie, working in the garden, getting a massage, or taking a bath. Or maybe it's simply wrapping up in a blanket and watching reruns of *Seinfeld* or *Star Wars*. Allow yourself a break today to indulge in comfort.

4.

FEEL YOUR GRIEF

- Stay in touch with your feelings by leaning into them when you have the energy and space to do so. In practical terms, this means that when feelings come up, stop and feel them, share them with a friend, or write them down. Doing so helps you release your grief.

- Society teaches us that emotional pain is to be avoided, not embraced. It is only in moving toward pain and grief, however, that we can heal the wounds that come when we lose something significant.

- Be aware if you notice others telling you how well you are doing with your job loss, or if you don't feel much at all. Sometimes doing well means you are avoiding your pain, hiding your emotions, or experiencing some of the natural numbness that grief brings.

- Of course, it is important to pace yourself when you are allowing your grief and pain to surface. Sometimes, you'll need to distract yourself from the pain or set it aside for a bit so that you can still move through your day. We call this "dosing" your grief, and it's a helpful concept to remember as you move forward in your journey.

- As Helen Keller once said, "the only way to get to the other side of something is through it." Practice moving through your grief and pain rather than trying to go around it or ignore its presence.

CARPE DIEM

Today, find someone to talk with and share your
thoughts and emotions about your job loss.

5.

UNDERSTAND THE DIFFERENCE BETWEEN GRIEF AND MOURNING

• Grief is the constellation of internal thoughts and feelings you experience with loss. Mourning, however, is external. It is the actions or words you use to outwardly express your grief.

• You are grieving the loss of your job. But to move through your loss, you must mourn. If you grieve but don't mourn, you'll get stuck in depression, anger, or fear. Grief held in can cause fatigue, headaches, stomachaches, trouble sleeping, and depression.

• Get your grief out. Find ways to express it. When you do, you'll feel yourself begin to move through your grief and come back into life.

• Open up and give yourself permission to mourn. This might mean allowing yourself to cry, talk, write, or let out a scream when no one is around. Whatever works, do it.

• Mourning is a process. Don't be surprised if you need to do it for weeks, months, or even years. There's no timetable for how long it takes to mourn something you've lost. In our hurry-up society, we often feel pressure to get over things quickly and move on. Honor your need to take time to grieve and mourn.

CARPE DIEM

Tell your job loss story to someone today. Telling your story of loss over and over again is like taking a shower every day. It washes away the grime, at least for a while. Eventually, the telling of it will get less and less painful and hold less and less emotional charge.

6.

RECOGNIZE FEELINGS OF SHOCK

- You may find that you don't feel much of anything yet. If so, you might be in shock.

- Feelings of shock, numbness, and disbelief are common during the first days and even weeks following job loss. These feelings are nature's way of temporarily protecting you from the full reality of your loss. Like anesthesia, they help you survive the pain of early grief. If your loss shocked you to your core, it may be a blessing to feel numb.

- We often think, "I'll wake up and this will not have happened." Early grief can feel like being in a dream. Your emotions need time to catch up with what your mind has been told. Your body slows in response to this emotional shock. You may feel like you can't do much of anything.

- Feelings of passivity often go hand-in-hand with numbness. Maybe you feel child-like. Maybe you are neglecting your basic needs for food, water, and sleep

- Simple decisions are hard during shock. You may feel zero energy, focus, or motivation to start searching for a new job. If your friends or family urge you to make decisions, tell them you need time to absorb the shock before thinking ahead.

CARPE DIEM

If you are feeling numb, cancel any commitments that require concentration and decision-making. Let yourself regroup. Find a safe haven that you can retreat to for a few days or for a few hours each day.

7.

LISTEN TO YOUR BODY

- When we are grieving, we often feel bad physically. We experience fatigue, headaches and migraines, stress, high blood pressure, and even body aches and pains. These symptoms are messages that we need to slow down and turn inward toward our grief.

- If you are still in shock, your body will naturally slow down, and your senses will be numbed. Your body is wise in this slowing down. Well-intentioned people may try to divert you from honoring this slow-down. Society often expects us to take a day or two off, then immediately get busy trying to find the next job. Ignore these expectations and honor your need to go at your own pace.

- Stay in the present and focus on what you need to do to get through today rather than focusing on worries about tomorrow. Just "being" may be all you are up to right now.

- Take care of your body. Breathe in and breathe out. Get adequate rest. Eat healthy food. Drink plenty of liquids. Relax your body with naps and relaxation.

CARPE DIEM

Right now, lie on your back with your knees up, or sit with your back straight in a cross-legged position. Take 10 large, slow breaths—filling and emptying your lungs completely. When you finish, consider the essentials of what you need to do to just get through today.

8.

ASK FRIENDS AND FAMILY FOR HELP

- When you experience a major loss, you need love and support from others.

- Don't feel ashamed of your heightened dependence on others right now. If your loss was recent, you may feel the need to be around people and to talk about your job loss often. You may need help financially, with chores at home, or getting things organized for your job search. Take comfort in the thought that other people care about you and are available to help. Think of specific ways they can help you right now.

- Ask your family or friends for ongoing support and patience. Don't hesitate. Those who love and care for you truly want to help. You just need to ask. Tell them how they can best help you process your emotions and deal with your loss.

CARPE DIEM

Call your closest friend right now and tell him you need his help through the coming weeks and months. Ask him if he'll be on-call for you. Maybe you need to meet with him weekly to laugh together or have him listen to your wonderings.

9.

CUT YOURSELF SOME SLACK

- Sometimes, more than one loss happens in a short period of time. When this occurs we experience a pile-up of losses, leaving us feeling overwhelmed.

- Losses that add to the pile include:
    - The death of someone you love
    - Divorce
    - Physical illness, injury, or medical diagnosis for you or a family member
    - Loss of property due to fire, flood, or theft
    - Children going to college or leaving home
    - Foreclosure or a financial need to move
    - A friend or family member moving away
    - A child struggling with school or friends

- If you had another loss occur around the time you lost your job, you may be at risk for "loss overload." When losses pile up, your ability to cope is stretched beyond its limits. You may feel surrounded by loss and endings. Maybe you find yourself grieving one loss one minute, and another the next. It might be hard for you to find steady ground.

- Loss overload can make you feel like you are going crazy and that nothing is going right in your life. Rest assured, you are not going crazy. You are, however, in need of special care. Identify ways to cope with this pile-up of losses. Reach out to others to talk. See a counselor. Meet with a financial planner. Ask someone to help you with a task. Mostly, cut yourself some slack.

CARPE DIEM

Does it feel like everything is going wrong? If so, stop and make a list of all the things that are going right in your life. Even if the good things seem small compared to your job loss or other losses, making the list will remind you that there is still cause for gratitude and happiness.

10.

RELEASE TENSION

- When we experience loss, our bodies feel it. We can carry tension and not even notice. Take a moment to mentally scan how your body feels. Do your muscles feel tight around the temples? Are there knots in your shoulders or neck? Do you have a headache or lower back pain? By scanning your body and practicing a relaxation or tension-releasing exercise each day, you can ward off more serious aches and pains.

- To relax, start by finding a quiet place to sit comfortably. Take in a few deep breaths. Next, mentally focus on your left hand and repeat to yourself, "My left hand feels warm and heavy." Repeat this until your left hand truly begins to feel warm and heavy. Relax your right hand then sequentially focus on your arms, legs, feet, and other body parts until your whole body feels relaxed. Take deep breaths in and out as you do this exercise. If desired, purchase a relaxation CD that will guide you through a similar exercise.

- You can also do quicker tension-releasing exercises. For example, if you are spending a lot of time sitting at your computer, do head rolls to release neck tension. You don't want it to hurt, so go slowly and pause for 10 seconds on each side, and front and back. To release shoulder tension, stand up and reach for the top of the doorway with both hands. Feel the stretch for 10 seconds in your shoulders, back, and arms. If you body is stiff, try stretching in the shower—touch your toes and lift your arms over your head while the hot water softens your muscles.

CARPE DIEM

Try a relaxation technique or tension-releasing exercise. Notice the difference before and after in how your body feels.

11.

AVOID BIG DECISIONS

- Now is not the time to make big life changes or take on new commitments. Your mind, body, and spirit are not ready for more.

- If you can (and this may not be possible), try to avoid making any major decisions for at least a few months following your job loss. Life changes, such as moving to a new house or a new city, getting divorced or remarried, may seem like proactive, positive steps. But often, such major upheavals only compound stress and delay the mourning of your job loss.

CARPE DIEM

Is someone pressuring you to decide something, today?
Ask her for time. Let her know that you are not in a
place to be making big decisions right now.

12.

LIVE SIMPLY

- Your plate is most likely pretty full during this trying time. Besides having a long to-do list, you may be feeling emotionally, spiritually, and physically drained.

- Keep your life simple right now. Do what you need to do to get through the day. Live moment-to-moment or hour-to-hour, if needed. Cancel unnecessary obligations. Minimize chores and tasks.

- Spend time with people you love, doing the things that give you pleasure. Eliminate or set limits with friends who drain you or make you feel worse when you're around them.

- Get out of the house. If being home is making you feel claustrophobic and stuck, get out and do something fun. Consider it a mini-vacation. What makes you happy? Take a stroll on a wooded path or peruse books at the bookstore. Go to the park and play fetch with the dog. It doesn't have to be a big event to serve as a break from stress. Guaranteed, you'll feel at least a little lighter by the end.

CARPE DIEM

Is there a commitment in your life that feels like a burden? Maybe it is a monthly club meeting or board position. Consider giving it up temporarily. Today, look into de-stressing your schedule.

13.

KNOW THE SIGNS OF DEPRESSION

- Feeling down or blue is normal when you experience a significant loss. But if your depressed mood lasts longer than two to three weeks and your feelings of anger, sadness, or hopelessness seem to be getting worse, consider getting professional help.

- Ask yourself the following questions to determine if you are experiencing depression:
  - Do I have little interest in things that would normally bring me pleasure?
  - Am I feeling down or depressed most of the time?
  - Am I having trouble falling asleep or staying asleep?
  - Is my energy level low, leaving me feeling tired?
  - Has my appetite changed significantly?
  - Do I feel like a failure or guilty for no good reason?
  - Am I having trouble concentrating or thinking clearly?
  - Am I moving more slowly, or do I feel fidgety?
  - Am I feeling a sense of hopelessness, or am I thinking about suicide?

- A yes answer to a few of these is expected after a job loss. Yet if you answered yes to several, it's time to seek help. Call a friend right now and tell her how you are feeling. If you can, meet with her today and let her help you figure out a plan to deal with your depression. Or, make an appointment with a counselor.

CARPE DIEM

Consider how you are feeling right now. If you feel
depressed, make a call for help. If you are feeling blue,
do something positive to shake up your mood.

14.

KNOW THE SIGNS OF ANXIETY

- Job loss is intensely stressful. You may be feeling a variety of physical reactions. With stress and anxiety, your fight-or-flight response gets activated—your blood pressure rises, your breathing accelerates, your heart rate increases, and your mind races. If it's hard to shut off this fight-or-flight response, you may be struggling with anxiety.

- You may also find it hard to sleep. Your appetite might change, and you might feel tense or agitated.

- Anxiety can result in a panic attack. A panic attack is a surge of overwhelming anxiety and fear. Panic attacks can cause several physical reactions—heart palpitations, shortness of breath, dizziness, lightheadedness, trembling, shaking, a feeling of choking, chest pain, fear of losing control, chills or hot flashes, disturbed thoughts, and more. Panic attacks often strike away from home, but they can happen anywhere and come on suddenly. They can happen once or repeat themselves.

- Know that you are not going crazy and that if you are having panic attacks, they won't harm your heart or threaten your life.

- To bust anxiety when it comes up fast and overwhelms you, try these tips: Look up at the ceiling, lower your shoulders, and take deep breaths. To slow your thinking, force yourself to think in complete sentences. Or, get up and dance, do jumping jacks, or run around the block for fast anxiety relief.

CARPE DIEM

Are you feeling anxious right now? Repeat these affirmations five times: "I am okay. I can handle this. A solution will come." As you do this, breathe slowly. Say one affirmation on each breath out.

15.

BE KIND TO YOURSELF

- You've been through a lot. You deserve kindness—from others but especially from yourself.

- Maybe you have the urge to beat yourself up for losing your job, thinking there is something you could have done differently. Put that self-questioning and self-judgment down. You don't have to carry it. There's a good chance that losing your job had less to do with you than it did with the inner workings of the company.

- To practice self-kindness, picture this: See yourself sitting on your bed, crying or feeling pain. Now, see yourself sitting next to yourself, putting your arm around the other you's shoulders. Rub her back as she cries. Sit together for a while.

- Be your own cheerleader. Get some sticky notes and write down a few positive phrases that have meaning for you, such as "I am strong. I can get through this." Put them on your fridge or bathroom mirror and read them several times a day. Also, make it a habit to celebrate small successes. Say "Good job!" out loud when you do something well, or pat yourself on the back, literally.

- Review your skills, talents, abilities, and personal strengths to remind yourself that you're capable.

CARPE DIEM

What are you beating yourself up about these days? Take a moment to answer that question. Now, see it as a bag of trash. Picture yourself picking it up and carrying it out to the curb. See the trash guys come and throw it in the truck. Hear the crunching as it's destroyed. Turn around and walk back to the house and sigh with relief that it's gone.

16.

ASK WHY

- Major life transitions, including job loss, often leave us questioning the meaning and purpose of life. Even if you have faith that things will turn out, you have still lost something that you value. It's normal to feel dumbfounded and have a desire to ask why.

- Why questions can surface uncontrollably and often precede How questions. "Why did this happen?" often comes before "How will I survive this?" It's normal to ask questions like:
  - Why this, why now?
  - Why me?
  - Why did it have to happen this way?
  - Why am I here, in this place of job loss?
  - Why do good things have to come to an end?

- The answers will come from within. You may decide that there is no answer to some of these questions. Your job loss may never make complete sense to you, and that's okay.

CARPE DIEM

Write down a list of Why questions that you have about your job loss. Explore these with someone you trust—someone who will let you ask without feeling a need to answer.

17.

LOOK AT WHAT YOU'VE REALLY LOST

- It's time to get real about the job that you lost. Bring your old job to mind. What were the parts of it that you disliked? What did you put off or dread doing? Reflect on the ways you were dissatisfied with your old job. Consider the people, the environment, and the principles of the company. Think about these questions:

  - What problems, pressures, restrictions, or unhealthy work conditions existed?
  - Did you feel respected and supported by your supervisor and coworkers? Did you have to compromise your integrity? Were your talents recognized and your hard work appreciated? Were you proud of the company and your work?
  - Did you feel harassed or even discriminated against? In what ways did you routinely live with mental or physical stress?
  - Were you paid what you were worth? Were the benefits good or lacking in some way? Were you given a fair amount of tasks or were you expected to wear too many hats? Did you ever consider leaving?

- The object of this exercise isn't to get negative about your old job but to allow you to see the big picture. It helps to put your job loss in perspective—being asked to leave stripped you of your control over the situation. Realizing that you might not choose your job again, if given the chance, helps you regain a sense of power and control over your career.

CARPE DIEM

Get a pen and paper and write down what came up for you when you did the exercise above. What were the main ways you felt dissatisfied in your old job? What characteristics do you want your future workplace to have?

18.

SEE THE BIG PICTURE
OF THE ECONOMY

- Job loss is often a direct result of the shortcomings of our current economy and the effect it has had on companies' money-saving measures and staffing numbers. Layoffs are increasingly common with today's globalization, increased competition, and economic downturn.

- The modern workplace has changed dramatically. Seldom do we see the stable, so-called "womb to tomb" employment. Rarely do companies offer pension plans that pay out well beyond retirement. Even a solid healthcare plan—that doesn't cost the employee thousands of dollars a year—is hard to find. Instead of lifetime jobs, we are experiencing what feels more like "free agent" employment.

- Beginning in the 1990s, the American workplace experienced unprecedented turbulence. Virtually every large and small corporation in America, from manufacturing companies to healthcare organizations, joined the ranks of companies that were forced to downsize. The increase in downsizing came about because of:
    - Advances and changes in technology
    - Outsourcing to other countries (to save money)
    - The economic downturn of the global economy

- Companies often view a reduction in the workforce as a disposal issue. In other words, to the company, it's not personal. But to you, it's very personal.

CARPE DIEM

Consider the economic or organizational reasons
that contributed to you losing your job.

19.

REMEMBER YOUR ACCOMPLISHMENTS ON THE JOB

- When thinking about your job, it's easy to focus on what went wrong or how it ended. Yet, no doubt, you accomplished a lot during the time you were there. Actively remember the people you impacted, the accomplishments you made, and commemorate the hard work that you did. By focusing on the big picture, you will be able to see the ending as just one of your experiences there.

- Remembering the past makes hoping for the future possible.

- Consider hard memories as they arise during this process. Try seeing them from several perspectives, not just the one you are used to. If you received a poor mark for performance at one time, think about what else was happening in your life or with workplace dynamics that influenced the poor mark. This will help widen your perspective about your job.

- Remember that you still have all the skills, knowledge, and talent you had before your job loss. Although you may be a former marketing director or machinist, despite your current unemployment, you still have those skills. They will not disintegrate or vanish.

CARPE DIEM

Take 15 minutes and make a list of the major accomplishments you had at your job. Consider all types—not just the Employee of the Year award, but the secretary you shared a joke with each morning, making her day a little brighter. Read the list to a family member or friend.

20.

ACCEPT THE REALITY OF YOUR LOSS

- It may be hard to believe, but you've lost your job. This may be one of the most difficult realities you have ever had to accept, depending on how long you had your job and how much you valued it. Yet gently, slowly, and patiently you must embrace the reality that your life has changed and that there is no going back.

- When you suddenly experience loss, you'll first try to make sense of it cognitively, on an intellectual level. Over time, you'll come to accept and acknowledge your loss at a deeper level. The shock of it might be replaced by feelings of sadness, disappointment, confusion, and worry about the future. You may also feel excitement and hope for new opportunities.

- Don't be surprised if you volley back and forth between acceptance and hope, and shock and despair. This might happen by the hour or by the day. On the days you feel lighter, take small steps to move forward. On the days you feel down, find ways to comfort yourself.

- Write out a response to this prompt: I used to be _____. Now that I have lost my job as a _____, I am _____. This makes me feel _____. Keep writing as long as you want to express your feelings about this change.

CARPE DIEM

Change your old morning routine to help you accept that today is different than yesterday. Add a morning walk and enjoy the crisp air or read out of a daily inspiration book.

CENTRAL NEED 2:

ALLOW YOURSELF TO MOURN

Your job loss has thrown you for a loop, but you've accepted that it happened. Now it's time to mourn—to move through the many emotions you are having. You'll find release in crying, venting, playing, cranking the tunes, and meeting with supportive people. It's also time to get still and allow yourself room to be where you are—to allow the movement of mourning to work, so you can move toward a new beginning.

21.

GIVE YOURSELF PERMISSION TO MOURN

"The unemployed haven't lost their jobs; they know where they are. Their jobs are now overseas or can be found listed proudly as efficiency accomplishments in the résumés of corporate executives. So I haven't lost my job. My job died."
—Mary Jo Purcell, unemployed American, Newsweek

- This life transition is similar to what you would experience if someone you loved died. Recognize that job loss is a kind of death. When you lost your job, you experienced the death of the:
  - Role you held within your company or organization
  - Job that was a core part of your identity and self-esteem
  - Career that you spent time, energy, and money building
  - Routine that created the structure for your everyday life
  - Daily interactions with certain people

- It's important to openly and actively mourn the death of your job. Try not to distract yourself from your feelings or deny that you have them.

- We all know that when we avoid feeling something, it comes out sideways. Sometimes, stuffing our feelings results in losing patience with our children or spouse, finding ourselves irritated about little inconveniences, or crying and not really knowing why.

- As you outwardly express your grief in healthy ways you will begin to feel the weight of the loss lighten. You will begin to pass through your pain.

CARPE DIEM

Write down the feelings you have over your job loss. Think about the outward way that you express these feelings. How else might you outwardly express them? Try doing so, today.

22.

NAME WHAT YOU ARE FEELING

- It is natural to feel emotions of anger, worry, worthlessness, and despair during this time of transition. You may feel lost and alone. You may feel out of sync with others around you.

- Sometimes, emotions come in waves making them difficult to identify. Learning to name your feelings helps you tame them. As Shakespeare's Macbeth said, "Give sorrow words: the grief that does not speak whispers with o'er-fraught heart, and bids it to break."

- Here are a few ways to identify and label feelings that you may be experiencing:

    - Sit still with no distractions. Ask yourself, "What am I feeling?" Breathe slowly and let yourself experience what arises. Or, take the opposite approach. Crank up music, listen, and express yourself by yelling or singing along loudly. See what emotions arise.
    - Give your feelings a voice. Try to prompt your feelings by saying: "I feel angry today because…." or "I could cry today, about…."
    - Ask yourself what you are feeling while driving in the car, taking a shower, or right after you wake up. These are times when unfettered feelings tend to surface.
    - Write a "Dear Job" letter to your old position or your previous employer that expresses how it feels to not have them in your life anymore.

CARPE DIEM

Search the internet for information about grief responses and see if any of the emotions you read about ring true for you.

23.

MAKE TIME FOR PAINFUL EMOTIONS

- Embracing painful emotions is not something anyone wants to do. Why feel pain? It hurts and it feels hard. It's easier to avoid, repress, or push away the pain of grief than it is to confront and embrace it. Yet, to heal and move forward, you will eventually need to feel the pain, grief, discouragement, anger, or sadness that you are feeling.

- While you do need to embrace the pain of your loss, you must do it in doses over time. Ask yourself how you feel about your job loss and share or write about what comes up—then take a break. You can't take in the enormity of your loss all at once. It's healthy to seek distraction and allow yourself breaks for pleasure and comfort each day.

- Consider ways that you distract yourself from your feelings. Are you on the internet for hours on end? Are you reading one novel after the other? Watching television constantly? Drinking too much? If so, make a conscious effort to hit the off button to allow your emotions space to come forward.

CARPE DIEM

Take a walk, ride a bike, or go to the gym. Doing something physical helps you release emotions. Or sit outside and stare at the trees and listen to the birds sing. When feelings come up, resist pushing or reasoning them away.

24.

GET HEALTHY ABOUT YOUR ANGER

- Anger often comes up when we experience a personal crisis. Anger is a completely normal human emotion. But when it gets out of control, it can cause problems at work, in relationships, and in your own sense of contentment and quality of life.

- Anger can mask other emotions; sometimes when we experience certain emotions, we feel anger instead. Emotions that sometimes disguise as anger are disappointment, fear, frustration, rejection, resentment, and feeling disrespected.

- There are a few ways to deal with anger when it arises. One is to express it. Anger that is expressed assertively, not aggressively, brings relief and helps us get our needs met. Another is to calm ourselves down by walking away from the situation, taking a mental break, and slowing our breathing and heartbeat.

- Actively express your anger by venting to a friend or former colleague, writing down your feelings, giving anger shape and form in art, and exercising. If needed, see a certified counselor.

- Anger that is held in can cause heart disease, stroke, depression, and substance abuse. It can also leave you feeling cynical and hostile toward others. If you carry emotions like anger into your interviews or a new position, employers will feel it. Take steps to actively resolve and express feelings of bitterness, anger, and resentment as you mourn this loss.

CARPE DIEM

Choose one of these methods for expressing anger
and spend some time doing it, today.

25.

VENT YOUR FRUSTRATION

- Frustration is defined as "dissatisfaction arising from unresolved problems or unfulfilled needs." Of course you feel frustrated. You are living in limbo, and your work and career are currently unresolved and unfulfilled.

- Similar to anger, frustration is a natural feeling that surfaces during job transitions. When frustration is not expressed, it can accumulate and lead to symptoms of anxiety and depression.

- There are a number of things you may feel frustrated about, including the:
    - Way your termination or layoff was handled
    - Lack of available positions that will offer you comparable pay
    - Shattered belief that if you work hard, things will work out
    - High rate of unemployment in your community
    - Loss of other benefits

- Expressing frustration in a safe, constructive manner is essential so that you don't carry it into your interactions with your children, your spouse, or your next employer.

- Expressing frustration often involves venting—getting it out. Try writing, talking, punching a bag, creating art, doing sprints up a hill, or joining an exercise class that lets you act out—such as kickboxing, boxing, karate, or even Zumba. Frustration that's released dissipates.

CARPE DIEM

What are you feeling frustrated about right now? Take a moment to write down your top 10 frustrations and find someone who will listen without comment or advice as you read them out loud.

26.

PROTECT YOUR FAMILY FROM STRESS

- Your unemployment has likely created some unexpected changes for everyone in your home. Your stress is contagious and can spread to your family, much like a cold or flu. Only you can prevent it from spreading.

- Watch for signs that your stress is spreading to your spouse and kids. Do you:
    - Talk about financial worries in front of your children?
    - Snap and react versus think and reason?
    - Skip important family obligations because you feel too pressured to stay home and work on finding a job?

- Here are a few ways to protect your family from stress:
    - Set aside family time at least weekly to enjoy each other.
    - Ask your family to tell you when they feel your job-search stress.
    - Create a clear separation between your job search and your family time.
    - Keep your life balanced. Ask for help when you feel overwhelmed.

CARPE DIEM

Let your family know that you value them through actions and words.

27.

GET YOUR DENIAL IN CHECK

- During the first few weeks following your job loss, you may naturally use denial as a way to protect yourself from the pain of losing your job. This is expected. As humans, we can only take in so much at one time.

- Yet denial can continue beyond what's healthy. Some ways you might be continuing to deny your job loss include:
  - Maintaining a lifestyle without having the financial means to sustain it
  - Feigning to go to work and concealing your lack of employment from your spouse
  - Not telling friends or extended family members about your job loss

- Denying that a problem exists helps us suppress our pain. Yet when denial is our primary coping mechanism, problems result in new problems, additional pressure, chronic stress, and more fear.

- The solution to prolonged denial is allowing yourself to feel your pain and frustration. If you do this, even in doses, the intensity of the pain you are feeling will fade over time. Allow yourself to confront your stress and pain, today. It will go a long way in reestablishing yourself.

- Every day, acknowledge the reality that you are unemployed and embrace your painful emotions. Describe your reality out loud to yourself or someone else.

CARPE DIEM

To flush out denial, ask yourself: What am I most
afraid of happening? Think about ways you can feel
secure in your life, right now, around this fear.

28.

CRY

- To mourn, you need to let your emotions out. There's no better way to do that than crying. Crying is release. Crying is letting down your guard and fully exposing yourself in the moment. After crying, you feel calmer and more settled.

- Tears are essential to mourning—the ultimate act of bringing what's inside, out. Tears release stress, pain, and worry. They are sacred and purifying. Don't be afraid to cry.

- You may find yourself crying at unexpected times or places. We call these "griefbursts." They are a natural part of the grief experience.

- As a society we're not so good at witnessing others in pain, so you may find that friends or family are uncomfortable with your tears. Try to find someone who is not afraid to sit with you while you cry.

- Keep in mind that not everyone cries during times of loss or hardship. The inability to cry is not a deficit and does not indicate that something is wrong with you. Instead, release emotions by exercising, writing, and talking with others.

CARPE DIEM

Sometimes we need a good cry. Find a way to trigger your emotions (watch a sad movie or write about what you are feeling) and release them through crying. Or, simply be open to crying when the urge comes.

29.

QUIET YOUR MIND

- Does your mind feel full? It's normal to feel anxious about job loss, but racing thoughts and worries can overwhelm you. Buddhists call this churning mental chaos "papanca," or monkey mind. This stressful jumping from thought-to-thought resembles a monkey jumping from tree limb to tree limb.

- To combat this monkey mind, we must use our body's natural relaxation response. One basic technique is clearing your mind. With daily practice, it can help you feel refreshed, more energetic.

- Try these techniques to clear your mind:
  - Find a quiet place that will allow you to practice in peace. Sit, loosen any tight clothing, kick off your shoes, and relax your body into a comfortable position.
  - Close your eyes and begin to breathe slowly. Monitor your deep breaths with a hand on your stomach.
  - Mentally focus on one peaceful word, thought, or image. If other thoughts should enter your mind, just relax, breathe deeply, and try again. Spend at least several minutes with your mind focused on this peaceful sensation.
  - Stretch and exhale to complete the exercise.

CARPE DIEM

In our busy world it's hard to find time to enjoy quiet and uninterrupted solace, but we can make the conscious choice to relax and clear our minds. Set aside 5 to 10 minutes daily to practice clearing your mind.

30.

PRACTICE NON-JUDGMENT

- Expect several emotions to surface in the coming weeks and months. Don't be surprise if you feel numb, angry, frustrated, scared, worried, lost, confused, and perhaps deeply sad. You may feel emotions all at once, or move from one to the other. Don't judge yourself about what you are feeling.

- As strange or uncomfortable as your feelings are, they are an important part of the grief process. Your feelings are not right or wrong, good or bad, they simply are. Allow yourself to feel whatever surfaces without judging yourself.

- Don't beat yourself up about not finding another job right away. After all, rushing into something that isn't a good fit will only cause more problems later on. Keep in mind that it takes the average American four to seven months to find a new job after losing one.

- As your feelings surface, say a mantra to yourself that fosters self-compassion and non-judgment. You can try one of these, or make one up that fits:
  - My feelings are necessary. They allow me to mourn this loss.
  - Feeling my emotions now will help me move to a new future.
  - I am in the muck of my feelings right now, and that's okay. Soon I will be on dry ground.

CARPE DIEM

Make a "feelings collage" with images from magazines and feeling words. Display it somewhere that you'll be able to reflect on it without judgment. When you see it, say to yourself, "I am feeling all sorts of feelings these days."

31.

START A JOURNAL

- Writing is a healing process. Psychologist James Pennebaker explains that, "Not only is the pen mightier than the sword, it can be mightier than the army of anxieties that keep us captive to stress."

- Writing about your job loss can help you openly and actively mourn. Putting your loss experience on paper helps to:
  - Give voice to your emotions
  - Process your feelings
  - Create a meaningful story about your job loss
  - Release tension through words
  - Gain new perspective
  - Feel a sense of control
  - See progress in your journey
  - Sort through the Hows and Whys of your job loss

- If you don't know where to start with writing, get your thoughts flowing with a "writing web." Get a piece of paper and make a circle in the middle. Write down a main thought in the circle that you want to explore—maybe it is simply "job loss" or a feeling, like "sadness." Now, draw a line to another circle. In that circle, write the first thought that comes to mind. If you have related thoughts about the new concept in the new circle, draw more lines to new circles and fill them up. Or, go back to your main circle and generate a new idea or thought. If one idea really sparks your interest, start writing about it on the side of the paper. Don't worry about punctuation, spelling, or making complete sentences—instead let thoughts flow in phrases, words, or doodles.

CARPE DIEM

Keep a daily journal on your computer or in a notebook and commit to writing in it at least a few minutes each day.

32.

REVITALIZE YOUR BODILY SYSTEMS

- Your body has absorbed the stress of your job loss, and it needs special care. Your nervous system and immune system have been especially taxed.

- Your nervous system has been working overtime, managing the fight-or-flight response that kicks in with stress. Your heart responds to this nervous energy by working harder. Even if you are slowing down on the outside, on the inside your body is working overtime. Your pulse and blood pressure are elevated, and your adrenals are working hard to regulate your stress hormones.

- When we are stressed, our immune systems are less able to make protective white blood cells. Keep in mind that colds and minor infections may be more common—it may take longer for you to recover.

- To keep your bodily systems running well, take care of your body with healthy food, water, and rest. Calm your systems and keep them strong with regular exercise and stress reduction techniques.

- Start taking a good multi-vitamin/mineral supplement to support your body right now. Consider taking extra B vitamins, which get depleted when we are under stress and are needed to provide us with energy.

CARPE DIEM

Set an appointment with your doctor to talk about ways you can support your body right now. Ask her to run some lab tests to check how your basic systems are functioning.

33.

MAKE CONTACT WITH OTHER PEOPLE

- Now is the time to rely on friends, family, and others for support. You don't have to go through this alone. Having support helps you to ward off isolation, express your feelings, and define your needs.

- Take a minute to identify at least five people who could actively support you right now. Consider:
    - Immediate and extended family members
    - Members in your church or the church leader
    - People at your gym or a place where you volunteer
    - Members of clubs or activities
    - Neighbors
    - Friends, including old friends you have lost touch with
    - Counselor
    - Former colleague that you considered a confidant

- If you are worried that people are too busy, make getting together convenient for them. Meet at a location that's near their work or home for a quick cup of coffee before or after work, for lunch, or a short walk on a nearby bike path.

- If the people you lean on for support have never experienced job loss, they may struggle to say the right thing and may inadvertently say things that don't feel very helpful (for example, "You just need to get a job."). Remember, their intentions are good, but it's okay to remind them that you don't need them to fix your problem.

CARPE DIEM

Don't be afraid to be specific about what your needs are and how they can best help you. Right now, think of at least three specific ways others could help you.

34.

GET STILL

- As Rainer Maria Rilke once observed, "Everything is gestation and then bringing forth." Sitting in stillness with your grief will help you honor your deeper voice of quiet wisdom. Create opportunities for moments of stillness and reflection. Where can you go to get still? Try these ideas:

    - Bring a blanket to a park and sit under a tree.
    - Drive to a favorite wooded trail and take a quiet, slow hike.
    - Sit on your porch or back deck in the sun.
    - Go to a coffee shop and find a cozy spot.
    - Take a bubble bath with candles and bath salts.
    - Attend a yoga class or go to a meditation center.
    - Hike to the top of a hill and sit and look at the vista.
    - Sit in a church or synagogue.

- Creating stillness is good for our spirits. If we don't calm down at a deep level now and then, we move through life feeling disconnected, uncertain, aimless, and rushed. Without stillness, our bodies, minds, and spirits don't have time to rest and rejuvenate.

- You may feel like you need to get moving without realizing that getting still is a vital part of that forward movement. Frantic attempts to quickly "move forward," "get past this" or "let go of the pain" are often counterproductive.

- It is through sitting with stillness that your soul is ever so slowly restored. Stillness is a teacher of contentment and peace.

CARPE DIEM

Right now, take a few moments to simply sit and be still. Close your eyes and become aware of the stillness. Hear the distant noises around you. See the light penetrating your eyelids. Lean back and relax into it.

35.

FIND A SUPPORT GROUP

- If you feel overwhelmed and alone in your job loss, consider joining a support group. Support groups provide a comfortable setting where people express their feelings and encourage each other.

- Support groups allow you to breathe a sigh of relief in knowing that you are not alone in your loss and your feelings. They help you get clear on what steps you need to take to heal from your job loss and move forward.

- Consider looking for a job loss support group through your local:
  - Hospital
  - Newspaper
  - Meet-up groups (www.meetup.com)
  - Community mental health center
  - Crisis or resource center or united way
  - Churches
  - Private counselors or psychologists

- If you are struggling with other stressful issues on top of coping with the loss of your job (like a chronic illness, alcohol or drug use, the death of someone loved, or divorce), consider finding a support group focused on that issue, instead. You will still find support and gain insight about your job loss, but it's most helpful to work on your core issue first.

CARPE DIEM

Call a few counselors today and ask if they know of a local job loss support group. If they don't, call the mental health center in your community or your area United Way.

36.

ENJOY NATURE

- The beauty of nature has a way of facilitating healing. Seeing the wonders of nature reminds you that there is still beauty, peace, and harmony in the world when you are struggling with your job loss.

- In some ways, we all suffer from nature-deficit disorder. We need time to explore and connect to the Earth. When we spend much of our time indoors, we don't get the chance to stimulate our senses as we do when we are outdoors. Studies show that when people experience the environment around them, they feel less stressed and depressed.

- Sunlight is a powerful healer. Less daylight during the fall and winter months is known to cause seasonal affective disorder (SAD)—a clinical type of depression. One solution to SAD is light therapy. Sunlight is the original light therapy, helping to lighten our moods and give our bodies doses of healthy vitamin D.

- Release the buildup of adrenaline and stress hormones you carry in your body by exercising in nature. By exercising, you'll also boost your immunity and lessen your depression—two proven outcomes of regular exercise.

- Our country has amazing national, state, and city parks, along with breathtaking national forests and recreational areas. Hiking trails, streams, and bike paths are waiting to help you embrace the healing force of nature.

CARPE DIEM

Pick a nearby natural area and take a hike or ride a
bike. While you are out, feel, smell, and experience the
healing powers of the nature that surrounds you.

37.

GET IN TOUCH WITH YOUR SPIRITUAL SIDE

- Your mind, body, and spirit are interconnected. When you neglect one area of your being, others are affected. Spiritual needs are often more difficult to recognize than physical and mental needs.

- The grief of job loss can bring on a spiritual crisis. When you are in spiritual crisis, you find yourself asking why questions and reevaluating the purpose and meaning of your life and things you value.

- Find answers to your spirit's questions and needs through:
  - Prayer
  - Prayer groups, bible studies, or conversations with your clergy
  - Support groups
  - Mindfulness—paying attention to what you are thinking and feeling in the moment, without judgment
  - Attending religious services
  - Contemplative practices like meditation or yoga

- Invite your spirit to come forth through a spiritual practice that works for you.

CARPE DIEM

Take a few minutes to consider your spirit and what it needs. Give it a voice by engaging in some form of contemplative practice.

38.

GET WET

- Many people find water to have a natural healing quality. Water soothes the body and the soul. When we spend time near water, we connect to its tranquility and flow.

- How to get wet? Here are some ideas:
    - Visit the ocean and experience its ebb and flow.
    - Take a hike to a mountain stream or waterfall.
    - Sit by a quiet pond or lake.
    - Visit a hot springs.
    - Soak in a hot tub, bath, or long shower.
    - Float in a city pool or nearby lake.
    - Fill a baby pool in your backyard and lie in it.
    - Walk in the rain.
    - Run through the sprinkler with your kids.

- Breaking water releases negative ions. Negative ions have been found to purify the air, kill bacteria, and increase energy levels.

- Water is one of the earth's four elements, a provider of life. It's pure and precious and brings healing when we experience it. Seek out opportunities to be near water whenever possible.

CARPE DIEM

Make a date with yourself to experience water in the next day or two.

39.

CRANK UP THE TUNES

- Music has been called the language of the soul. Music gives voice to our emotions. Experiencing music is an effective, fun way to mourn.

- While we listen to and move with music, we feel the tension in our bodies release. We feel our hearts and spirits surge.

- All types of music can be healing—rock-and-roll, classical, blues, folk. It just depends on what speaks to you.

- If you can, don't just listen to music, experience it. Sing along while you drive—even at the top of your lungs. Dance and move your body while you're alone in your living room, or initiate spontaneous family dance sessions. Go and listen to a band. If you play an instrument, pick it up and jam—with others, if possible. Really get into it.

- Consider making play lists that elicit different emotions. Make one of songs that energize and motivate you, another of songs that help you contemplate life.

- Revisit old music that once spoke to you. There may be whole albums that played a part in a significant period of your life. Play them and get in tune with your emotions.

CARPE DIEM

Visit a music store today and sample a few CDs or tracks. Buy yourself something that resonates with what you are experiencing right now.

40.

PLAY

- Ah, to unabashedly play. Wasn't it great when we were kids and all we had to do most days after school or during the summer was to play? Our minds were free. We didn't have big worries like making a living, paying bills, or saving for retirement. We just were. Present. In the moment. Just being.

- Yet kids don't own the corner on play. We adults can play, too. How long has it been since you:
  - Waded in a stream
  - Ran through the sprinkler
  - Jumped into a pile of leaves
  - Shuffled barefoot across freshly mown grass
  - Built a sandcastle
  - Blew bubbles
  - Jumped rope
  - Visited a toy or candy store
  - Flew a kite
  - Climbed a tree
  - Shot hoops
  - Played on the teeter-totter or swing

- If pretending to be a kid again feels too foreign, think of ways you like to play as an adult. Go skiing or snowboarding, swim in the ocean, dig your feet in the sand, go camping, make a fire, or watch a football game.

CARPE DIEM

Right now, leave your serious adult self behind. Go
do one of your favorite childhood activities.

41.

FIND A THIN PLACE TO MOURN

- In the Celtic tradition, a "thin place" is where the physical world and the spiritual world meet. There is a Celtic saying that heaven and earth are only three feet apart, and in the thin places, that distance is even smaller.

- Thin places are where the veil between the holy and the everyday is so thin that when you witness it you intuitively experience a sense that you are not bound by time or space. Thin places can be experienced outdoors where:

  - Water and land meet
  - Land and sky come together
  - The river meets the riverbank
  - The beach and the ocean collide
  - The mountain touches the clouds

- It may take some physical exertion to get to these places, but it is well worth it. There's a good chance that your spirit will feel at peace, your mind will feel calm, and your body will feel grounded. Once you are there, pray, walk, talk out loud, write, breathe, or simply sit in the presence of the moment. Allow the grief you are experiencing to join you, and express itself.

CARPE DIEM

Do you remember experiencing a thin place in your past? Where was it? Get in touch with that memory. Better yet, revisit the place if possible.

CENTRAL NEED 3:

SET YOUR INTENTION

Your intention is like a seed. Remember planting a bean seed in a milk carton in kindergarten? The seed started out dry, hard, and inflexible. It was almost impossible to imagine that it held the potential for green. Yet, as you nurtured it, you saw that it did. It broke ground and revealed a ball of soft, green promise. In this section, you'll foster your seed of intention. You'll get in touch with the purpose behind your actions, thoughts, and beliefs. You'll open to new growth, new opportunities, and become prepared to take action and begin your job search.

42.

LIVE WITH INTENTION

- Intention. It's a word that's been tossed around a lot lately in self-help settings. What does it mean to live with intention? To start, it means to live with purpose.

- To live with intention, we must first take a personal inventory. We must become aware of the thoughts, actions, behaviors, and beliefs that fill our minds and days. Then, we consciously choose which ones we want to keep around. When a negative or unhelpful thought comes up, we counter it with a positive thought. We don't fight it. Instead, we quietly disregard it and choose to think otherwise.

- To live with intention is to be decisive. You decide the type of person you want to be instead of automatically responding to what others want you to be. You decide what makes you happy and you start bringing that into your life.

- Living with intention is about knowing yourself. What brings you pleasure and joy? What are you innately good at doing? What are you interested in?

CARPE DIEM

Where to start? Commit to simply observing yourself for a little bit each day. Hear your thoughts and notice your reactions to things as you move through your day.

43.

FIND YOUR CENTER

- What does it mean to be centered or to find your center? It means to experience that self-assured place where you feel calm in your spirit and in who you are. You feel grounded.

- Centering allows you to let go of resistance and release fear. It keeps your focus on the big picture of your life. When you are centered, small annoyances don't bother you since you are not as susceptible to reacting to the external world.

- When you are un-centered, you are more likely to feel agitated, irritated, judgmental, and lost. Little things get to you and have the power to radically alter your mood and motivation. You are like a fallen leaf that gets blown this way and that way in the wind. You might feel lost inside and therefore actively seek something outside yourself to fill you up. This is a dangerous place—one that lets bad habits and addictions reign.

- When you are centered, you are more aware. You have more clarity, focus, and calmness. Your intuition is easier to hear and follow. You have more faith in yourself and your future.

- Find a centering exercise that works for you. Consider meditation, yoga, mindful breathing, guided visualizations, or affirmations. Some people get centered through exercise, being outside, going to a support group, seeing a counselor, and basking in the presence of their loved ones.

CARPE DIEM

Today, call a friend who is hope-filled and centered and avoid a friend who is negative, cynical, and un-centered. Set the intention to hang around with people who are centered.

44.

BE MINDFUL

- What is mindfulness? Like the word intention, it's one we are hearing a lot lately, even though the practice of mindfulness has been around for centuries, originating from Buddhism. Mindfulness is about staying present and focusing on the here and now. It's about being aware, without judgment, of what is going on inside of us. It's about staying in the moment.

- Practice mindfulness by becoming aware of the thoughts that are walking around in your head. If there's a guy making snide remarks about your abilities, just watch him walk on by. Simply be aware of him, without starting a fight or feeling the need to defend yourself. Once you have a good idea of the general thoughts floating around in your head, you can figure a way to encourage them if they are positive, or counteract them if they are negative.

- Mindfulness also requires tuning in to your body. Notice your breathing. Feel the sensations you are having in your body right now. Make a conscious effort to clear your mind. In this way, it is like meditation.

- If sitting still in a meditative position is not your style, you can practice mindfulness at any time during the day by focusing on the task at hand and clearing your mind. Try it while you fold laundry, garden, paint a wall, walk the dog, or stand in the check-out line. The result will be that you feel calmer and more centered.

CARPE DIEM

While you complete a task that's on your to-do list today,
do it mindfully. Focus on the task and nothing else.

45.

ASK WHAT DIRECTION YOU'RE GOING

- It's good to stop now and then and think about the direction that you're heading. This will help keep you heading more directly toward your life goals and will guide your daily choices.

- Stop and ask yourself some big picture questions. What do you want to bring into your life? What dreams, convictions, talents, and qualities are waiting to be revealed? What aspects of yourself have you abandoned because you were focused on making a living? Here are some other questions to consider:

    - Am I happy with my life? If not, what needs to change?
    - Does my lifestyle fit who I am?
    - What brings me the most satisfaction in the work that I do?
    - Is my work meaningful to me?
    - What do I value most in life? How do I honor these values?
    - How well do I create balance in my life?
    - What brings a sense of meaning and purpose to my daily life?

CARPE DIEM

Take a mental inventory of how you spend your time. Is most of your time spent supporting your values, desires, and interests? Or do you need to do some adjusting?

46.

PRACTICE SELF-CARE

- Living with intent includes taking care of yourself on every level—physical, emotional, cognitive, social, and spiritual. There are 8 basic ways to practice good self-care:
    1. Eat a balanced diet of nutrient-rich foods and get good sleep.
    2. Exercise regularly, including at least three cardio workouts a week.
    3. Play, have fun, and enjoy life.
    4. Listen to music, dance, chant, or play an instrument.
    5. Receive and give love and touch.
    6. Express your creativity through interests and hobbies.
    7. Experience nature regularly.
    8. Practice your faith or spiritual beliefs.

- By engaging in these healing practices regularly, you'll keep your life balanced and you'll feel more centered, focused, and able to move forward.

CARPE DIEM

From the above list, determine which practices you are doing and which you're not. Take a moment to write out a brief daily action plan on how you can incorporate each of these practices.

47.

GET GOOD SLEEP

- Set an intention to get good rest. Some people take the attitude that sleep is overrated. It's not. Studies show that when people are sleep-deprived, they are much more likely to be depressed, irritated, accident-prone, and unhealthy.

- Most adults need at least eight hours of sleep a night to feel like they can function the next day. Some need more, and a few need less. Figure out how much you need and aim to get it.

- Practice good sleep hygiene, which includes:
    - Setting a regular sleep and waking time
    - Avoiding exercise before bed
    - Making your room dark
    - Eating light and not snacking before bed
    - Limiting caffeine and alcohol, and avoiding nicotine—all three are known to disturb sleep
    - Having a bedtime routine that promotes quietness and winding down (don't put a television in your room or do work in bed)

- If you are having trouble sleeping, empty your mind of worries by filling out "worry cards" before bed. Get a stack of note cards and write one worry on each card. For example, you might write: "I need to update my résumé." After you write down your main worries, set the cards down and say, "I can do this tomorrow" or, "I will get to this soon."

CARPE DIEM

Tonight, start a new bedtime routine that is focused on de-stressing.
Take your phone off the hook, bathe or shower, listen to soothing
music, and sip hot herbal tea in bed as you read a good book.

48.

START A HEALTHY HABIT

- We all have something we could do to improve our health. Maybe it is getting our heart-rate up regularly with cardio exercise, lifting weights to keep our bones and muscles strong, or eating less junk food. Vow to start a new, good habit for your health, today.

- Consider these new-habit ideas:
  - Increase your water intake. According to the Mayo Clinic, water flushes toxins out of vital organs, carries nutrients to your cells, and provides a moist environment for ear, nose, and throat tissues. The clinic advises people to drink eight glasses of water a day. Remind yourself to drink water regularly. Make a simple rule, as in always having a water glass or bottle with you.
  - Limit your alcohol intake. Maybe you got in the habit of drinking alcohol to numb the pain of your job loss. There are healthy limits to alcohol intake, and it's important to stay within these limits. Seek help if you have more than two drinks a day consistently. Also, become aware of the reasons you drink. See if you can replace drinking with a healthier habit—such as drinking hot tea or staying sober to tuck your kids into bed.
  - Work out every day. A new exercise habit doesn't need to be earth-shattering. Start slow and build up. You don't need to join a gym and vow to go five days a week. Instead, set a goal to move your body every day. Maybe it's just a walk around the block one day and 20 minutes of floor exercises the next.

CARPE DIEM

What habit can you start today to support your
body and commit to living healthy?

49.

GIVE YOURSELF A BOOST

- With job loss, we feel deflated. It can feel like a part of us has been stripped away. Make a conscious effort to take some of that power and energy back. Give your self-esteem a boost, today.

- Boost your self-esteem by doing something you are good at or something that is a passion of yours. It could be something you gave up when you had kids or when you started working full-time. Maybe it's photography, writing, watching documentaries, or reading poetry.

- Explore a new activity or interest that intrigues you. It doesn't have to be a big thing, like skydiving. It can be as simple as visiting a bookstore and finding a magazine with an interesting focus. Or looking through your recreation department's pamphlet of upcoming events and classes and signing up for one.

- Help someone or volunteer. Again, no long-term commitment required. Maybe you love bike racing or running. Volunteer to work the water stations for an upcoming race. Or sign up to build trails or pick up trash for the parks department. Better yet, tutor a child or volunteer at a day shelter. Helping others is proven to boost our own moods and feelings of self-worth.

CARPE DIEM

Take a minute to think about what intrigues you. If you are drawing a blank, think about interests you had in high school or college. What have you always wanted to try but never had the chance? Can you take steps toward trying it, today?

50.

REFLECT ON YOUR LIFE

- Think about the story of your life. Consider who you were as a child—the skills, characteristics, and insights that you had. Now, consider yourself as a young adult, when the world held such promise. What were some of the things you vowed to do in your life? What really lit your fire? Finally, move into your adult years. Think about times of intense growth and change, and times you laid low.

- Your life story has led you to the point where you are now. Did you live intently, setting a course? Or did you go along with the flow of events that landed you here? Regardless of whether your course was straight and intentional or flowed from side-to-side, you made decisions along the way. You gained wisdom and grew into who you are today.

- Are you the person you hoped you'd be? Have you reached some of the goals that you had along the way? Give yourself credit for your achievements. Smile about the good times. And for those times you wished you'd done differently, release them from your mind. Vow to forgive yourself for the things that keep you stuck.

- You determine your course from here on out. You decide your future, no one else. There is no direction but forward. Reflect on what you want to bring into your future and consider the steps you need to take to realize your intentions.

CARPE DIEM

Schedule 15 minutes of solitude into your day today (and tomorrow, and the rest of the week). Go for a walk, sit somewhere quiet, or lie in the sun on the rug. Reflect on your life.

51.

LISTEN TO YOUR INTUITION

- During times of transition, our spirits want to be heard. One way they speak is through intuition. Intuition is that quiet, centered voice that guides us. It comes as a gut feeling—that something feels right or wrong. It comes as a hunch. It comes in dreams. Or, it speaks through premonitions and déjà vu and gives us a glimpse into something in advance. However it comes, it feels like the truth.

- Often, your logical mind will doubt your intuition because it might promote the opposite of what seems to "makes sense." Since your logical mind is louder and bossier, your intuition might get drowned out. But when you go with your intuition, your decision seems right and certain, even if it doesn't logically add up.

- Explore these avenues to open to your intuition:
  - Record your dreams. Have a pen and paper next to your bed for right when you wake up. Your intuition tries to speak to you through dreams. If you have repetitive dreams, or very vivid dreams, pay extra attention. It means your spirit is trying extra hard to get a message across. Writing out your dreams can make their meaning more obvious and reveal patterns.
  - Let go of fear. When you are calm, your intuition gets through. Do a centering activity that works for you to release fear and get relaxed.
  - Empty your mind. Do this through meditation or writing. Again, whatever works for you.
  - Catch your split-second thoughts. What comes up before logic starts to speak? Is your gut feeling positive and inviting or negative and leery? Trust these emotions.

CARPE DIEM

Go to the library and get a book or research on the internet to learn how to interpret the symbols in your dreams.

52.

LAUGH EVERY DAY

- Humor is one of the best things in life. Laughter brings hope and healing. It helps us see that we often take ourselves too seriously. It instantly lightens our moods.

- Laughter truly is the best medicine. Studies show that laughter reduces stress hormones in our bodies and increases endorphins and neurotransmitters that improve our health. Research proves that laughter strengthens our immune systems and increases our tolerances for pain.

- Allow yourself to laugh. Yes, things have been tough, but laughter doesn't diminish that. You can laugh and still do the work you need to be doing to heal, mourn, and search for a new job. Taking breaks to laugh and play reenergizes you as you move forward.

- Remember the fun times you shared with the people at work, their sense of humor, their grins, and the sound of their laughter.

- Consider the idea of acting "as if." It may seem false at first to act as if your life is fine, and the burden of finding a job isn't weighing you down. But after a while, if you act happy and laugh a lot, you might find yourself beginning to grow into the part of a happy, hopeful, and positive person.

CARPE DIEM

Invite laughter into your life today. Call a friend who always has a joke, watch a show that makes you giggle, or get silly with your kids.

53.

LIVE LIFE WITH MEANING

- When we're in transition, we often scrutinize our lives. It's natural to take a close look at our choices, actions, state of being, and lifestyle.

- Define what makes your life meaningful. If your relationships bring you meaning, find ways every day to feed them. If finding challenging, well-paying work brings you meaning, take steps this afternoon to bring that forth. To figure out what brings you meaning, ask yourself these questions:
    - What gives me a sense of purpose?
    - What makes waking up worthwhile?
    - What activities fulfill me?

- To get a sense of what brings you meaning, look at your past. What experiences did you have that stand out as meaningful? What experiences gave you a heightened sense of being alive? Consider periods when time flew by quickly or you felt like you made a difference. Exploring these tell you what you value, and living your values brings meaning.

- If you find your attitude slipping, and you begin to feel like this job search is a burden that you must do, rather than something you want to and can do, it's time to redirect your attitude. Get out of the bog and start moving forward again.

CARPE DIEM

Look through old pictures to gain a sense of what brings
your life meaning. Write down what you discover.

54.

SEE THE GOOD IN CHANGE

- Good often comes from change. Yet, the good can be hard to see. All we know at the start is that our routine has been disrupted and we have to learn and try new things—things that are still a mystery to us. It's hard to believe that this forced change might actually bring new opportunities, joy, and reward.

- When people are asked, "Which made you grow more, the hard times or the good times you've had?" almost everyone says the hard times. It's true. When we face challenges, we are forced to use new skills and tap into abilities we may not have known that we had. This strengthens us.

- You might not be ready to see the possible good in this job loss yet, but it exists. You will have a new future. And maybe, it will be better. You have been handed a chance to redefine or change your career if you want.

- Job losses sometimes serve as motivation to start a business, return to school, or gain training in a field you've wanted to explore. If you make a move from a career or job that left you unsatisfied to one that you like, your life will improve.

CARPE DIEM

Let yourself daydream about which jobs seem appealing to you and why. Don't limit yourself to ones that are within your current skill or educational level. Pay close attention to your answers when you ask why something appeals. These can give insight into what kind of job, career, or workplace environment you hope to find next.

CENTRAL NEED 4:
TAKE ACTION

Remember when your milk-carton bean began to grow? Every day, you could see its progress. It quickly became taller, stockier, and stronger. Soon it was branching out leaves. Its growth was rapid as it headed with amazing speed toward what it was to become. By taking action, you affirm your intentions. You create your future. This section provides you with a number of practical ways to actively prepare for, and carry out, your job search.

55.

SET UP A PLACE TO WORK

- You've come a long way. You've gotten through the shock of your job loss and accepted that it's real. You're grieving and mourning. You're living with intention. Now it's time to take action. Start by setting up the physical space where you'll work.

- Complete these steps to create a productive work space:
  - Choose a location where you have everything you'll need within arm's reach. This may be your home office or a desk in the family room. Or, you might need to create a portable office with your laptop, cell phone, and a portable file case for your supplies to work in a coffee shop or the local library—especially if you are using a public computer.
  - Make a list of office supplies so that you can create good workflow once you get started. Get yourself pens, notepads, envelopes & stamps, file folders, printer cartridges, sticky notes, a stapler, and other supplies.
  - Set a hands-off rule for anyone else in the house so you know your space won't to be tampered with, unless it's the kitchen table. Even then, stake out your ground for the time you are using it.
  - Establish an electronic or paper file system. Start with a main folder labeled "Job_Search_2011." From there, you can have sub-folders entitled "resume_coverletters," "strategicplan_vision," "leads," "contacts," and others.

CARPE DIEM

Post inspiring quotes and affirmations in your work space.
Make it as comfortable and you-focused as possible.

56.

TAKE INVENTORY OF YOUR SKILLS

- We don't lose skills. Once we have them, they stay with us. We might need a quick refresher now and then, but that's it. The skills and talents you had before you lost your job are still yours. You'll take them with you into your next job.

- Take a thorough, written inventory of your skills by listing your:
  - Personal strengths, skills, and talents. Picture yourself at your last job, and the ones before that. What did you do well, day-to-day? What did your supervisors praise you for during job reviews? What did other people ask you to do?
  - Work-related achievements and accomplishments. What were the big projects you worked on? What specifically did you contribute? What did you do above and beyond your job requirements—or what did you do especially well? Get specific.
  - Roles you played. A go-to guy? A troubleshooter? A good team player? Think beyond the labels. Don't just write a general descriptor; write down evidence to back it up.
  - People skills. Were you well-liked? Did customers respect you?
  - Challenges. What challenges did you overcome or turn around? What skills did you apply?

- Create your inventory in your journal or save it in a file under "resume_prep_inventory."

CARPE DIEM

Post your personal inventory somewhere you can see it.
It will serve as a reminder of all you are and all you've
accomplished. It can also be a quick reference for
unexpected call-backs on your résumé or application.

57.

CREATE A STRATEGIC PLAN, PART 1

- It may sound like overkill to write a strategic plan for your job search. It isn't. A strategic plan is simply a thought-out approach on where you are now (Part 1), where you want to go (your vision statement, coming up next), and how you'll get there (strategic plan, Part 2). It is setting an intention, on paper, for your job search. Besides, you can use these ideas again in your résumé and cover letters.

- First, think about where you are. Strategic plans have mission statements that state a purpose, list values, and inventory strengths and talents (your Inventory).

- Purpose statement. Jot down what your purpose is in this job search—what's the ideal title you hope to hold? What are others you will consider? What jobs are you qualified for? What jobs are you interested in—even if they are outside your usual realm?

- Values. What type of company do you want to work for? Consider its values, work style, benefits, size, reputation, and work environment. For example, can you work in a cubicle? Do you want to work for a big, established corporation or a small startup? Now, turn your attention inward. What workplace values do you want to uphold? What matters to you—flexibility, good benefits, team spirit, having support to succeed, a positive work environment?

- Try not to be overly practical. Dream a little. Write down your ideals. Your strategic plan will serve as a roadmap over the next few weeks and months. You'll find it especially useful if you are pursuing a new career path or direction.

CARPE DIEM

Pull out pen and paper or get on your computer
and begin your strategic plan.

58.

WRITE A VISION STATEMENT

- Your vision statement is about getting clear on what you want. It helps you see the big picture of your career path and job search.

- Consider these questions:
    - If anything were possible, what would I want my next job/career to look like? How would I want it to be different from my old job?
    - What do I want to be responsible for in my job/career? What types of challenges do I want to face? What elements will keep me motivated and interested?
    - What traits do I hope that my boss/coworkers/team possess?
    - What salary range do I deserve based on my experience and skills? What is my greatest hope regarding salary? What am I willing to work for?

- If you are unclear, try expressing what you don't want. You might say, "I don't want a long commute." Or, "I really dislike cubicles." This will help you state what you do want.

CARPE DIEM

Create faith in your vision. When you finish writing, stop and close your eyes. See yourself in a new workplace that is the ideal of what you envisioned. See yourself smiling, happy, and productive. Revel in the details.

59.

CREATE A STRATEGIC PLAN, PART 2

- You've considered your mission and vision statement. You're almost done. The final part of your plan is setting strategic objectives and goals.

- Consider what you need to do to carry out your mission and vision. Make a plan of action. Set your strategy. What steps do you need to take to get from here to there? Here are some ideas:
  - Identify at least three ways you will access open positions (e.g., newspaper, specific online sites, networking). Meet with your contacts regularly.
  - What's your daily plan? Will you make two calls a day to inquire on positions? Set up an informational interview each week? Send out two résumés a week? Post your résumé on reputable sites? Search trade journals? Set realistic daily goals.
  - You'll need your job-search tools on hand. On what date do you plan to have your résumé done? Your personal commercial prepared? Your references? Get out a calendar and set some dates.
  - Set up a few people to be your job search supporters—they can listen to your pitch, practice interview questions with you, and hold you accountable to goals.

- Work in ways to reward yourself. If you apply for three jobs in a week, give yourself a free pass to take an afternoon off for fun. Stay balanced.

CARPE DIEM

Pat yourself on the back! You've finished your
strategic plan for your job search.

60.

GO IN A NEW DIRECTION

- Maybe your strategic planning made you realize that you want a career change. If so, you have more thinking to do. Here are some ideas on how to change your career or go in a new direction, courtesy of business consultants Anne Barber and Lynne Waymon:

    - Go up. Maybe you are ready to be the boss. If so, find a mentor and drill him about his job and how he got to where he is. Ask him to review your Inventory to see if you have the skills and experience for a position like his.
    - Go back. Did you stray away from your original goals when you first set out? Maybe that was a good thing, but maybe it wasn't. Maybe you realize you'd rather be the teacher than the principal or the writer than the editor. When you do something that's satisfying, you'll have success.
    - Go sideways. Look for lateral moves—positions that are similar to your old one. Consider internal customers or employees who did a similar job to yours. If you know some from your old job, meet with them for ideas.
    - Go over. Jump the fence and make contact with outside suppliers, customers, and vendors from your old job. You already know their needs and they know your character and competence. Consider becoming a consultant or an independent sales representative for them.

CARPE DIEM

Take a minute to think outside the box of your current career or job. What other careers require similar skills and experience as yours? What appeals?

61.

STEP OUT OF THE ORDINARY

- If traditional paths for your career appear blocked or stagnant, you may want to consider non-traditional alternatives or a combination of these. Here are a few ideas:
  - Go home. Many career skills can be used to start a home business. These include writing, speaking, teaching, selling, computer engineering, software design, graphic design, GSI work, and others. Explore companies that hire telecommuters and contract employees or put projects out for bid.
  - Go somewhere else. Is moving an option or does it hold appeal? Relocating to an area with more job opportunities or a lower cost-of-living may be wise.
  - Go temp. Temporary placement is available in many jobs, even white-collar jobs. Temp positions can serve as a foot-in-the-door and lead to a permanent opportunity.
  - Go part-time. Consider part-time work even if you need more pay. Again, part-time work can lead to more hours and eventually become full-time.
  - Go narrow. Are you an expert in your area? Consider becoming a consultant. Fees for consultants can be attractive, and this option offers flexibility and independence.

CARPE DIEM

It's easy to get stuck into thinking there is only one way to do your career. Call a few knowledgeable people in your field and ask them to brainstorm ideas with you on alternative career avenues.

62.

WATCH OUT FOR SCAMS

- Wanting a new job so badly can make you vulnerable to scams that promise you the world but deliver little.

- Here are a few things to watch for:
  - Ads in local and national periodicals for agencies asking for payment for job searching or starting a business. While there are decent headhunters out there, these folks give you nothing in return, just minimal replies from companies with no openings or a starter package of overpriced goods.
  - "Work at home" opportunities. Be careful if they ask you to pay for supplies up-front or make an investment. They often give little in return.
  - If you are having difficulty getting a loan, be careful of con-artists who run "credit clearing" services. They ask for a fee but supply you with minimal changes to your credit rating—often just giving you information that's already public. They rarely contact a lender for a loan.
  - Multilevel marketing. These virtual companies sell goods and services through distributors with different rates at different levels. Think twice, even if others urge you to get involved. Often you have to put money up-front for products, and if you can't sell them, you lose the money and are stuck with the product.

CARPE DIEM

Stop and ask yourself, "Am I feeling desperate right now?" Re-read your inventory and strategic plan. Remind yourself what you want.

63.

TAKE A STEP BACK

- How much time should you spend on your job search? The short answer is as much as you can. But it can be mentally draining, and you might become ineffective if you work at it full time. Be realistic and pick the time when the house is quiet and you are most alert. Set a schedule and stick to it. When you complete your goals for the day, take a break.

- As with any long-term goal, it is helpful to set milestones along the way—times you check in on your progress, weekly, or monthly. Reward yourself when you've met your goals.

- Your state of mind is paramount, and a job search can be tiring. Be aware of mental exhaustion. When you are spent, don't spin your wheels. Allow some time to refresh. Keep regular exercise and social connection in your routine.

CARPE DIEM

Take a minute to stop and reconsider the big picture of your job search. Make sure you've built in positive reinforcements along the way.

64.

POST YOUR STRATEGIC PLAN

- It's important to revisit your strategic plan regularly. Consider this plan to be your personal job search map.

- Print it out and post it on a bulletin board in your office area or on your fridge. Include your inventory. Highlight key items so they catch your eye, or write them out separately as a list of quick bullet points. Look at these every day as you sit down to work or make your morning coffee.

- Set a goal to revisit your strategic plan monthly. See if it is still relevant or if parts of it need deleting or adding. What timelines and milestones need adjusting? Are there other strategies you can add that you've discovered along the way? Are you making progress? If not, what's holding you back? Add specifics.

- Maybe you realize that you need to rewrite your strategic plan now that you have more insight. This is especially true if you've changed career directions.

CARPE DIEM

Revisit your strategic plan by creating a vision poster. As you think about your future job, cut out images and words from magazines. Glue them together in a collage. Let your poster reflect your ideal vision of what your new job will be. Hang it on your wall.

65.

TRACK YOUR PROGRESS

- It's important to note and keep track of your progress each day. Not only is it motivating to see what you've done, it helps guide you as you move through your job search.

- Develop a daily system to track your progress. This might include:
  - Logging your daily activity. On an online or paper calendar, make a bullet list of your daily job-search accomplishments. Include where and to whom you sent résumés, what calls you made, etc.
  - Keeping a running list of contacts and potential leads. As you search, you'll come across names of people and companies of interest. Maybe you read about a new company coming to town in the business section of your local paper, or one that's expanding. Maybe an old colleague gave you a few names of people to contact.
  - Log your appointments. Keep a calendar with the various appointments you make related to your job search. These might include networking meetings, interviews, or visits to potential employers.

CARPE DIEM

Get out your calendar and back-log activities from the last
few weeks. This gives you a sense of accomplishment.

66.

STRUCTURE YOUR DAYS

- Having a daily plan keeps us moving. It gives us reason to get out of bed in the morning.

- Create a daily plan to keep you motivated. Here are some ideas:
    - Write out an agenda for the day. Include daily goals and ideas on reaching those goals. When scheduling appointments, set them for times you tend to be most alert and clear.
    - Dress for success. Shower and groom before sitting down to job search. This is your work right now.
    - Do the top three hardest items on your daily list first. Getting these behind you will relieve anxiety and stress as well as move you forward.

- Build in motivation by starting tomorrow's list today. It will help you get started, without stalling.

CARPE DIEM

What do you need to do that you've been putting off? Do that, today.

67.

DON'T GET STUCK IN THE MUCK

- Even with the best intentions, we all slip sometimes. Maybe you've reverted to feeling the pain and shock of your job loss. Maybe you are feeling discouraged by your seeming lack of progress.

- Job searches are hard. They challenge our beliefs of self-worth. They make us start thinking that there's nowhere that we fit. Continual rejection wears down our belief in our strategic plan. These thoughts can spiral us into immobilization.

- Is it difficult to get up in the morning? Is your personal hygiene slipping? Do you wear your pajamas all day? Are you distracting yourself by watching daytime television or YouTube videos? Worse yet, are you spending money you don't have? If so, you need to take action to shake up this state. Right now, go to your desk and do one new thing to move forward. Make that call you've been putting off. Set up an informational interview. Ask for a tour of a company you are interested in working for, or call their human resource department and inquire about openings. Take one big action to jumpstart your job search. If it doesn't turn out, don't worry about it. Focus on your action, not the results.

- If you truly feel stuck, call a friend. Tell him how you feel and ask him to brainstorm ideas with you. Maybe something he says will spark an idea to get you back on track with your daily goals.

CARPE DIEM

Make a list of one action you can take each day for
the rest of the week. Put it on your calendar.

68.

KEEP LEARNING

- While you job search, keep learning about things of interest inside and outside your field.

- Consider these opportunities to learn more about your career area:
  - Apprenticeship or job shadow. If you know someone who has mastered a job that you'd like to explore, ask if you can work alongside her for a day or on-and-off for a week.
  - Learn by listening to audiotapes, CDs, podcasts, and internet videos. Look for resources focused on job searching, marketing yourself, and networking. Or explore ones that discuss new advances in your area of expertise.
  - Audit a college class. Even if you don't want to earn credits toward a degree, you can complete a college course, simply to learn. This is called auditing a class. Check out what courses are offered at a nearby, or online, college or university. The cost is usually less than if you take it for credit.
  - Review the competition. Study companies similar to ones you worked for in the past—even ones located out of your area. This will give you a better sense of your industry and upcoming trends, strengthening your interview discussions.
  - Register for a vocational class. Look to religious, civic, and community organizations, or try an online correspondence course.

- Explore learning opportunities outside your area of study as well. If there is another career path that you are interested in, take a related class or research it on the internet.

CARPE DIEM

Are there gaps in your skills or knowledge of your industry? Research ways to fill them, today.

69.

TAKE CHARGE OF YOUR FINANCES

- Finances are never a fun topic, especially while job searching. While it may feel hard, analyzing your financial situation will help you gain more control over your money.

- Draw up a monthly budget. Look at what goes out, and what comes in. List your hard bills—those things that don't change like mortgage or rent, and the trash bill. Now, list your soft bills—those expenses that flex a bit each month, like groceries, gas, and household supplies. Figure out what you spend on your soft bills on average by looking through past bank statements. Compare these totals to what is coming in.

- Now, go through your records and examine your personal spending. Look at costs for entertainment, dining out, clothing, and travel. See if you can identify areas of waste.

- If you are carrying debt, consider visiting with a credit counseling agency that is affiliated with regulating agencies such as the NFCC (National Foundation for Credit Counseling). One option is the non-profit Consumer Credit Counseling Service (1-800-388-2227). Credit counseling agencies help to consolidate debt and work with creditors.

- If your house is in danger of foreclosure, call your lender immediately. Often, they can arrange an alternate payment plan. For counseling on avoiding foreclosure, contact a government HUD-approved housing counseling agency at 1-800-569-4287. Watch out for foreclosure recovery scams.

CARPE DIEM

Take the time today to analyze your expenses and income sources.

70.

FIND WAYS TO SAVE MONEY

- First, get real about your spending. It's hard to swallow that with a job loss often comes a change in lifestyle and spending.

- Move into economic survival mode. Try these tips or seek the advise of a financial planner or credit counselor:
  - Apply right away for unemployment benefits to maximize your length of support. Plan on spending the entire day applying and take along a pay stub, W-2 form, a dismissal notice, your Social Security card, the company's business name, address and IRS identification number, and something to read.
  - Your severance pay should be viewed as bridge money to be managed carefully. It is not a good idea to pay off mortgage debt or credit cards if you have no other reserve.
  - Begin to redefine what you see as the good life. Look for lifestyle changes. Maybe you pull the kids from daycare while you are unemployed, eat out less, or penny-pinch at the grocery store.
  - Make it difficult to make impulse buys. Don't carry credit cards. Use cash; you'll spend less. When you grocery shop, go on a full stomach and stick to your list.
  - If your expenses clearly outweigh your earnings, explore solutions. Are there things you can cut or temporarily put on hold? Maybe you are making automatic payments to your kids' college funds. Maybe you are carrying more minutes on your cell phone than you actually use.

CARPE DIEM

Start a new money-saving habit, like brewing coffee
at home or clipping grocery store coupons.

71.

FIND EXTRA INCOME

- Need extra money? You have more options than you might think for making money right now. Consider these:
  - Pick up temp or seasonal work. Find out which stores in your area are doing inventory and apply to do it temporarily. Is it near the holidays? Apply for temp work in retail stores or holiday events.
  - Start a home-maintenance business—rake lawns, shovel snow, do minor repairs, if your skills allow. Or, pet sit, do daycare, or use your office skills of accounting, data entry, writing, or marketing. If your kids are old enough, get them involved. Run a free ad on Craigslist and post flyers in your neighborhood.
  - Do you have items you can sell? How about that French door in the garage that never got installed or that road bike you bought and rarely used? Again, try Craigslist or eBay. If you have a lot of stuff, have a garage sale.
  - What did you used to do for a living? Consider getting an evening job waiting tables, bartending, or hostessing. Also, try retail stores for part-time work.
  - Can your spouse pick up extra hours right now?

- It can be a daunting task to try to manage without the paycheck that you are used to, but it may be doable if you reduce spending, manage and minimize debt, and pursue alternative sources of income.

CARPE DIEM

Ask your family to brainstorm ways you can save money. Look at ways that all family members can contribute to solve this family problem.

72.

NETWORK

- Before you cringe at the idea of networking, know this: 60 percent or more of jobs are found this way. The old saying that "it's who you know" is true for job searching.

- Get in the habit of networking all of the time. Sitting next to someone on a plane? Strike up a conversation and reveal you're looking for a job. You can network anywhere there are groups of people: church, neighborhood gatherings, holiday parties, community events, college alumni gatherings, organizational meetings, social clubs, and more. Don't forget the obvious—former coworkers, bosses, and business associates.

- Join a professional group—attend FACs (Friday Afternoon Clubs) at your local Better Business Bureau, or another business social or association meeting. Be selective. Only join groups that hold potential for making contacts with others in your line of work.

- Take a direct approach and ask for job leads, or be less direct and ask for advice or information. Also, impress by being an interested listener.

- Join an online career network. Many universities and even some high schools have career networks for alumni. Or locate one for individuals in your area of study.

- Make it a point to introduce yourself clearly and have a quick, one- or two-sentence response to what you do. You can add a reference to a major success, as in: "I work as a software engineer. I helped create the guts of Intel's latest processor."

CARPE DIEM

Have you been invited to a social gathering? Go. You never know who holds the connection to your next job.

73.

GET YOURSELF A PAGE

- Believe it or not, having a social network page like Twitter or Facebook can help you get a job. Perhaps not surprisingly, a 2010 study by Cross Tab Marketing found that 75 percent of companies research potential employees online before hiring. Eight out of ten companies say a positive online image influences their hiring.

- When making your page, consider what reputation you want to put across. Think of it as a chance to "brand" yourself, as it's called in marketing circles. Take some time to think about the image you want to give potential employers. Advertise your skills and on-the-job accomplishments.

- Social networking sites include Facebook, LinkedIn, Plaxo, and Twitter, among others. There are also blogs and podcasts on specific topics to join or experience—there are even forums specifically on job searching. Some social network pages have a strictly professional development focus such as LinkedIn. By befriending people in your area of business, you can create a network of resources for your job search. You can also get the latest news on advances in your field.

- If you have a page already, consider cleaning it up. You want to keep your online image as career-focused as possible.

- Check in with your social networks often, daily if possible.

CARPE DIEM

Create a page on a social networking site, today.

74.

ORGANIZE YOUR CONTACTS

- If you last updated your Rolodex in the 1990s, don't despair. After a little tinkering, and maybe help from a computer-savvy friend, you can set up address books of contacts on your computer, or even online.

- If you use Microsoft Office Outlook, you can store contacts there, but there are more specialized versions online. You can also find contact management software at any office supply store.

- Use these tips to keep your contact address book organized:
  - Organize your contacts by last name, first name, job title, company and phone, email, and fax information. In Outlook, there are tabs to enter several lines of information, so you can even take notes on when and where you spoke with them last, what was discussed, and any leads they may have offered.
  - Enter information for former employers, coworkers, business associates, clients, and suppliers. Every time you discuss your job search with someone who seems interested and holds potential, add them to your file.
  - Print a copy of your contact list so you can take it with you, if needed.

- Finally, you may want to pull out the modern version of the Rolodex—a business card holder, to store the business cards you collect.

CARPE DIEM

Use your computer's calendar software to
schedule networking as a daily activity.

75.

SEARCH FOR JOBS ONLINE

- One of the easiest places to look for jobs is online. There are many sites that offer not only databases of available jobs, but links to company websites, job boards, and company career pages. Many supply job searching tips, advice, and tools—like salary calculators.

- Job search sites let you post your résumé and apply for jobs. You can specify if you want your résumé to be viewed for a specific job opening, or by all potential employers.

- The following are a few of the better-known sites. Search by keywords (job titles), careers, and location.

  - monster.com
  - jobsearch.com
  - careerbuilder.com
  - career.com
  - justjobs.com
  - indeed.com

- Use a search engine to find a job, such as Google. Simply type in your job title and city and see what comes up.

- Visit the websites of companies you are interested in. Almost every large company, university, or organization lists job openings on their site. Also, check out professional organization websites in your area of interest—they often have job boards.

CARPE DIEM

Choose one of the sites listed above and search for a job in your field today. Post your résumé for potential employers to see. If needed, ask a friend or family member to help you.

76.

WRITE YOUR OWN COMMERCIAL

- Prepare a short summary of yourself that you can deliver with ease. Develop a one-minute commercial about yourself. You will use it frequently as you network, conduct phone inquiries, and interview for jobs.

- Pack your spiel with upbeat, descriptive language and solid examples. Consider the following:
  - Use a descriptive title to identify yourself and what you do. Some job titles are easily recognized, others are not. If yours is general, vague, or too technical, make it clearer. For example, instead of saying "development specialist," you could say, "I find funding for university programs and ventures. I work in development."
  - Describe the types of companies you work for and the customers you serve. For example, "I help start-up companies that focus on green products connect with investors." Potential employers want to know that you are customer-focused.
  - Share how you help your customers solve their problems. For example, "When the start-up companies are short on cash, I find hidden funding sources that they never imagined were there."
  - End with a recent success story. Companies want employees who can produce results. For example, "Last year I helped a group of professors get a grant from the National Science Foundation to continue their research on green energy sources." Success stories show that you can deliver.

CARPE DIEM

Develop a few different short summary commercials. One might emphasize your technical skills and another your people skills.

77.

WRITE A GREAT RÉSUMÉ

- Your résumé is your spiel on paper—but longer. Think of it as your ticket to an interview. Or your own personal brochure. Its purpose is to sell you.

- Today's résumés are much more than a chronological list of work experience and education. They go much beyond simple statements like "manage sales staff." They give specifics and boast achievements, as in "managed sales staff of 10, increased sales by 60 percent in 2009."

- Résumés typically have four sections—Professional Objective (or just Objective), Professional (or Work) Experience, Education, and References. A great addition to this list is the title Summary of Qualifications up front. It's where you showcase your top skills and strengths—backed up with real-life achievements—and tailor the résumé to the job. Include a subsection titled Strengths with a few key words, as in: "'Skilled manager," "Team player," "Workflow expert," followed by examples and numbers to prove each.

- Once you create your résumé, you're not done. Generic résumés that fit every job are passé. Tailor your résumé, even if it is just slightly, for each job. Change your objective to match the job's title, or get close to it. Add key words from the job description.

- Other tips include:
  - Use strong action words. Proofread. Be leery of using a flippant email address like crazylegs@ or hotlips@.
  - Keep it to two pages, front-back, if possible.

CARPE DIEM

There's a lot of good information on résumé writing on the internet. Do a search on "résumé writing tips" before sitting down to write your résumé.

78.

BE INTERVIEW-READY

- According to a well-known human resource expert, the first five minutes of the interview is what makes or breaks it. In that time, the interviewer has taken in your grooming, appearance, handshake, presence, ability to make eye contact, and has decided if you are articulate and if your personality fits with the company.

- When dressing for the interview, be conservative. No flowery skirts or tennis shoes, regardless of the company's dress code. Wear a clean, pressed, plain-colored suit (yes, women, too). Wear practical shoes and carry a briefcase.

- Get there early for last-minute review and to get calm. Before you walk through the door, breathe deeply. Practice positive self-talk: "I can do this. I am ready. I am calm." Breathe. Go a step further: visualize the interview going well the night before and think of that vision while you wait.

- Practice interview questions. Focus on questions that relate to the job description and support them with real-life examples. If they ask for someone who is a team player, have examples of when you played for the team and struck a home run.

- Get to know the company. When it fits, mention what you know in the interview.

CARPE DIEM

Devise answers to common interview questions, like "What are your long-term career goals?" and "What are your strengths, weaknesses?" Research others and prepare for them.

79.

INTERVIEW WITH CONFIDENCE

- Okay, you've arrived early. You've taken deep breaths and mentally pictured yourself in the interview being charming, articulate, and confident. Turn off your cell phone and sit up straight. Be ready to give that confident, firm handshake with warmth and a smile.

- You've made it through the door. Now, relax. Listen intently to questions and answer them directly with only relevant sidetracking. Interviews often follow a common format: They start with small talk then move to set questions about your education, work history, background, skills, experience, strengths, interests, and finally your career goals and philosophies.

- Focus on the questions and pause and think before answering. If needed, ask them to repeat the question. Be thoughtful. Be upbeat and positive and use examples to prove your point. Reference what you know about the company. Finally, pull out your question list and ask the ones that fit, along with others that arise during the interview.

- You've handed over your reference list and letters of recommendation (if available), given a final pitch of why they want to hire you, and thanked them for the interview. You're done, right? Not quite. When you get to the car, jot down notes about the company and the job to be used to write a thank-you letter.

CARPE DIEM

Think out a positive answer to "Why did you leave your old job?" If you were downsized, first say something positive about the company, then explain in simple terms what happened, as in "ABC was a great company to work for. Unfortunately they lost a major client and had to close my department." Keep your emotions in check.

80.

DON'T BE AFRAID TO BRAG

- Modesty is overrated, at least when it comes to job searching. Don't be afraid to brag. It's expected, and if it's done without too much bravado or narcissism, it will be well-received.

- Make sure your résumé, personal commercial, and interview prep and delivery are chock-full of success stories. Don't hesitate to err on the side of more versus less when describing your experiences. For example, if your title was assistant to the director, but in reality you performed director duties, say so. You could say, "My boss had great confidence in me, so she handed me entire projects, such as being in charge of the company retreat from start to finish." You can even make honest projections, such as "In many ways, she was grooming me for a position like hers."

CARPE DIEM

Practice bragging yourself up in front of the mirror.
Practice a confident but not audacious tone as you
describe why an employer would want to hire you.

81.

CONDUCT IMPRESSIVE PHONE INTERVIEWS

- Phone interviews are often used to weed out candidates or conduct out-of-town interviews. They are a little more challenging, as you've just got your voice to impress.

- Be prepared: Have your résumé on hand, notes on key points you want to make, and a pen and paper handy. Warm up your voice beforehand and have water nearby. Most importantly, schedule it when no one else is home.

- Writer William Bridges has coined the mnemonic "DATA" to remember when trying to impress a prospective future employer:
  - Desire. Say that you want the position, tell why, and explain why you are a great fit.
  - Abilities. Tell how you have what it takes to get the work done. Describe how you solved problems or achieved results in the past.
  - Temperament. Show a warm side to your personality. Tell how you got along with former coworkers and bosses.
  - Assets. Reveal your personal characteristics, experience or areas of expertise that make you stand out among the other candidates. Make them feel like they are getting a deal by hiring you.

- An effective phone interviewing technique is to try to match the interviewer's speaking style. Match their pitch, tone, and speed. You'll have instant rapport.

CARPE DIEM

Divide a sheet of paper into four sections. Write D in one, followed by A, T, and A. Enter statements that speak to your Desire, Abilities, Temperament, and Assets.

82.

LET YOUR REFERENCES
SPEAK FOR YOU

- Employers want the inside scoop, and they won't rely on just you to give it to them. That's why references are so important. Rarely is a job given without first checking references.

- You'll need to have three to six professional references. Ask associates (coworkers, colleagues, mentors, clients) and past supervisors—people you believe will give you a good recommendation—if they'll be a reference. If they say yes, consider asking them to write you a letter of recommendation, too. Avoid using friends, unless you are connected professionally.

- Your reference sheet needs to give current information and be updated regularly. List names, accurate titles, company names and addresses, direct phone numbers, and emails.

- Give it a great deal of thought about who to ask to be a reference. Think about who knows you best in regards to work style and job responsibilities. Who might best brag about your accomplishments and skills? Also, try to get a wide spectrum of associates as references so the employer can gain insight into all aspects of your abilities.

CARPE DIEM

Call a few associates today to see if they will represent you as a reference. Ask them to write a brief letter of recommendation, which you can hand out during an interview along with your references.

83.

REWARD YOURSELF

- Phew. You've been working hard. It's time to reward yourself.

- You might be feeling a lot of energy about your job search right now. You might feel inspired and pumped up. You might feel nervous. Take that energy and direct it into play or exercise.

- Purposefully turn your mind away from your job search. Forget about it for an afternoon or a day. Fill your mind with things that bring you joy or serenity. Re-explore some of the ideas in the second section of this book, such as Get wet, Crank up the tunes, and Play.

- You may feel guilt about having fun right now because you "should be" looking for a job. Are you saying things to yourself like, "If I have fun, it must mean that I am a slacker"? Are others pressuring you to stay on task? Realize that your job search cannot occur 24 hours a day/7 days a week.

- Celebrate! You are ready to enter the final phase of your job search—you're ready for your life to be transformed. You're ready to enter your new career.

CARPE DIEM

What do you enjoy doing? Do it today, or if it demands planning, set it up for a day this week.

CENTRAL NEED 5:

ALLOW FOR TRANSFORMATION

You set your intention to get a new job and you actively, and thoughtfully, tended to your job search. You've done your work and you're ready. Remember when your milk-carton bean of yesteryear reached full bloom? You took it home from school and planted it in fresh ground. It continued to grow until it was strong enough to withstand wind and rain because it knew what it was—a hard, dry seed—and what it had become—a fully alive plant, ready to bear fruit. Like your bean plant, your intentions and actions have taken root. You are ripe for getting a new job. You are ready to be transformed. Open to it, and know that it will happen.

84.

LET CHANGE IN

- The Chinese use two symbols for change—the symbol for crisis and the symbol for opportunity. Job loss sent you into crisis mode. But it has also opened new opportunities—possibilities that you may not have been able to see before.

- As you move toward transforming your work life, it is important to pay attention to opportunities that present themselves. Train your eye and mind to see opportunities—or more accurately—opportunities for opportunities.

- When we open to change and point our lives in a decided direction, we often have doors open or present themselves. Have you ever learned a word then began to see it everywhere? That's what happens when you open to opportunities. You'll get little signs pointing in the direction you want to go. Maybe one will come in the form of your friend mentioning off-handedly that a new company is relocating to your area or when you notice that an expert in your field is speaking at a conference next month. These are little invitations to action.

- Some people say, "It just fell in my lap," or "I am just naturally lucky." Don't be fooled. They first mentally, emotionally, and spiritually opened to having events turn out the way they did, guaranteed.

CARPE DIEM

Try this exercise. Stand up and open your arms wide. Gaze toward the sky. Say out loud, "I am open to change. I am ready for my new career to begin. I am open to opportunity."

85.

ADOPT A POSITIVE ATTITUDE

- There's a coping style used among transformational healers called an "attitude of hardiness." It's about accepting, head-on, what comes your way without flinching.

- With an attitude of hardiness you:
    - Refuse to see yourself as a victim
    - Believe you have power and influence over the events in your life
    - Feel a sense of control as things around you change
    - See the possibilities for personal growth
    - Feel a sense of hope
    - Muster the energy to actively engage rather than withdraw when times are difficult
    - Persevere in the face of rejection
    - See setbacks as steppingstones instead of obstacles
    - Keep the big picture in mind
    - Refuse to take things personally

- Attitude is a choice. Choose to move forward with a hardy attitude. It will result in a more meaningful and purpose-filled life.

CARPE DIEM

Have you applied for but not been accepted for a job recently?
Adopt an attitude of hardiness about the experience.

86.

BE DISCERNING

- With transformation comes a sense of personal power and the realization that you can influence the direction your life is going. Often, the journey from point A to point B involves several decisions along the way.

- Before making important decisions, stop and ask: "Is this decision congruent with who I am?" and "Does this decision move me forward?" Ask these questions for little decisions, too, as you move through your day.

- When you are discerning, you are using your intellectual, emotional, and spiritual powers to distinguish what is helpful and what is not in carrying out your strategic plan.

- Every major decision you make dramatically shapes your future. Yet, small decisions can't be made flippantly, either, because they add up to big decisions, whether you're aware of it or not. For example, deciding to abandon your job search for a day won't knock you off your path. But deciding to shirk on the next day and the next will— adding up to one big decision to put your job search on hold.

- During your job search, your decisions are influencing your finances, family, lifestyle, self-care, and career status. Influence them positively.

CARPE DIEM

Think about a few recent decisions you've made. Were they in line with your core values, beliefs, or strategic plan? If not, think about what you might decide differently, next time.

87.

DON'T JUST SURVIVE, THRIVE

- Those who have walked the path of job loss and gotten to the other side often share a simple but important message: You will not only survive, you'll thrive. Know this: your life can be full, rich, and satisfying if you choose to live intentionally and with meaning, rather than simply existing.

- You might slip back into times of thinking that you can't get through this. But you can, and you will. It may be difficult, but over time, and with a forward vision in mind, you will make it to the other side. Soon, your job loss won't be the first thing on your mind when you wake up in the morning. It will be getting ready for work.

- Trust that you will find your niche in the world. Your new job is out there, waiting for you. And it might just be better than you ever expected.

CARPE DIEM

Do you feel a need to reset your course? If so, it's time for a breather. Revisit Central Need 3: Living with Intention. Choose a few activities that appeal to you and do them.

88.

VOLUNTEER

"The greatest degree of inner tranquility comes from the development of love and compassion. The more we care for the happiness of others, the greater is our own sense of well-being."

—Tenzin Gyatso, the 14th Dalai Lama

- It may seem counterintuitive to volunteer when you have lost your job. Yet it has been proven that when we give to others, our own mood and motivation is improved. Volunteering can help you transform your life.

- You will be rewarded personally, and possibly professionally. Volunteering helps you:
  - Reconnect to your community in a meaningful way
  - Feel like you are contributing and making a difference
  - Recognize your value and your talents and give you the chance to use them
  - Keep you from feeling lonely or isolated
  - Build your social network
  - Provide networking opportunities
  - Gain new skills, especially important if the volunteer work fits with a new career path

CARPE DIEM

Explore a few volunteer opportunities in areas that interest you. Call your local United Way or check the newspaper for ideas.

89.

GO BACK TO THE BEGINNING

- If you are finding it hard to create a new beginning, it may be because you haven't finished your ending yet. It's been said, "You can't steal second base and keep your foot on first base."

- Go back and review Central Theme 2: Allow Yourself to Mourn. You must give yourself time to authentically mourn and emotionally integrate the loss of your job before you can truly commit to another. Since your job loss, have you take the time to:
  - Openly and actively mourn the losses you experienced?
  - Re-orient yourself and get grounded?
  - Self-reflect on what you need and want?
  - Renew your body, mind, and spirit?
  - Set your intention to heal?

- If you haven't, turn back to earlier pages and take the time to do this before you work on transformation. Transformation cannot be forced.

CARPE DIEM

If you are struggling to find your new beginning, ask yourself these questions: "Have I truly reconciled the loss of my old job?" "Do I have a sense of purpose, a vision, and a plan?" "Have I taken time to renew and transform myself?"

90.

KNOW THAT IT'S ALL YOU

- Ultimately, you are the only one in charge of your life. Understanding this, and integrating it, will help you transform your job loss from a life-altering experience to a life-enhancing one.

- Blame is immobilizing. If you still hold bitterness or blame about losing your job, explore these emotions. Revisit Central Need 2: Allow Yourself to Mourn. Do the work of exploring your emotions so that you can work through them and release them. Blaming takes away your personal power—something you need to believe in your future.

- As you look at your job loss, consider how you've contributed to getting where you are right now. Did you play a role in your job ending? Is there something you need to improve or change about yourself—your attitude, lifestyle, or career focus?

- Take the reins and accept that you, and only you, are responsible for how today, tomorrow, and your future unfolds. The beauty of realizing this is that it frees you to create the life that you want. You can make success happen.

CARPE DIEM

Is there anything you need to take responsibility for in your life? Take one action today to resolve a conflict in your personal or work life.

91.

KEEP PERSPECTIVE

- What does it mean to keep perspective? It means to keep your focus on the end goal. It means to not waver or bend with external blows. Keeping perspective is important during a job search and helps you more easily endure rejection and waiting.

- One way to keep perspective is to keep your emotions in check while job searching. Try not to get too wrapped up in the results. Think of every action you take as one step closer to your end goal, which is somewhere off on the horizon. If you stumble on a rock—say you get a rejection letter or a curt response to a phone inquiry—don't give it much thought. Look up. See the horizon and take the next step.

- If a lost opportunity spirals you down, consider why. What was the take-home message? Did it start old tapes in your head running that say you are not good enough, or that there's nothing out there for you? Try to see it for what it is.

- If every rejection feels like a big hit, you might want to re-explore, and then release, your beliefs about your job loss. Ask yourself: "What did my job loss say about me?" and "What toll is being unemployed having on me?" See what comes up. If you hear negative self-talk, find someone to chat with who can restore your perspective.

CARPE DIEM

Take a moment to write several answers to the question,
"Why did I lose my job?" Look to see if the list contains
answers that are self-sabotaging or empowering.

92.

DEFINE YOURSELF

- You are not what you do. It's easy to lose track of that along the way. Imagine defining yourself not by your job title or how much money you make but by who you are as a person. It may be funny to answer the question "What do you do?" with: "I do a lot of things. I'm a father. I volunteer at the local shelter. I love taking photos, watching football, and spending time with my family." But it'd be more honest.

- Maybe your work identity feeds your self-esteem and helps to define you, but it isn't you. Or at least all of you. Get in touch with who you are, as a whole being.

- One way to do that is to think about why you like other people. Is it their job title or material possessions? Or is it because they are loyal, honest, trustworthy, caring, make you laugh, and fun to be with?

- Funerals have a way of bringing this home, fast. When people stand up to talk about the person who died, rarely do they say how great she was at her job. Instead, they say how she loved her kids, was a good mother and friend, and volunteered at the food bank. These are the things that matter, in the end.

CARPE DIEM

Think about what you would like people to say about
you at your funeral. Then, consider ways you can
become—or continue being—that person.

93.

STAY IN THE MOMENT

- Living in the moment means being aware of what is happening within and around you, right now.

- It can be hard to set the past and future aside, especially when you are working toward a new future career, but if you can stay in the moment—and focus on what's in front of you—you will transcend fear and worry. You will be productive and make progress.

- When you learn how to fight off distractions and bring yourself into the moment, you'll be rewarded by feeling centered and calm.

- Take a moment to close your eyes and focus all of your attention on your breath—listen as your breath inhales and exhales. Do this for a while. Feel the oxygen going to your brain.

- Next, try to clear your mind. One way to do this is to sit back and watch your mind, as if it were a movie screen. See what images, thoughts, and words appear. If what you see is simply noise and nonsense, take note of it and continue watching. Becoming aware of thoughts can make them stop. To break thoughts, pull yourself back to the rhythm of your breathing.

- If you are feeling fear or another hard emotion, release it with your breath and inhale its opposite. For example, while you breathe, say, "Strength in; fear out." Or pick other words that apply.

CARPE DIEM

Make deep breathing a daily habit. Do it
whenever you feel tense or unfocused.

94.

ANCHOR YOURSELF

- Starting and ending each day with a centering exercise grounds and centers you. It helps you create and restore a sense of stability, security, inner peace, and harmony throughout your day. Anchoring exercises center your body and your mind.

- To center your body, close your eyes and bring all of your attention to the center of your body (your heart or stomach). Concentrate on filling these areas with your breath. As you breathe deeply, center your mind by reading a passage that speaks to you. Repeat it a few times. For example, this one by Mohammad feels cleansing and grounding:

> *Give me, I pray to thee*
> *light on my right hand*
> *and light on my left hand*
> *and light above me*
> *and light beneath me,*
> *Increase light within me*
> *and give me light*
> *and illuminate me.*
> —Mohammad

- Anchoring each day helps you to:
  - Release negative emotions and invite positive ones
  - Feel less anxious, stressed, and weighed down
  - Be filled with energy, creativity, and a sense of hopefulness

CARPE DIEM

Find a passage in a daily meditation book or book of spiritual or inspirational poems and musings that anchors you. Integrate this passage into a brief morning or evening ritual.

95.

TRANSFORM YOUR EMOTIONS

• Transformation literally means to experience a change in form. If you are experiencing emotions that are stalling you, actively transform them. Here's how:

- Transform your anger into energy. Write down the dissatisfying aspects of your last job. Use your answers to define what you want in your next job.
- Transform your fear into compassion. Close your eyes and envision yourself being compassionate with your past coworkers and colleagues. If it feels right, see yourself giving compassion to the person who let you go.
- Transform your pessimism into opportunities. Take your negative thoughts and turn them into optimistic, hope-filled statements. For example, if you are thinking, "I am not hirable," turn this into, "I am hirable. I just haven't found the right job, yet."
- Transform your workspace into something new. Relocate to a new area, or bring light into your space with new paint, pictures, flowers, or a desk lamp.

CARPE DIEM

Have you been having negative thoughts, lately? Bring one up and turn it into a positive. Repeat your new, positive thought as a mantra. You might not believe it at first, but with each repetition, it will gain power.

96.

VISUALIZE

- Visualizing is a powerful tool. Olympic athletes spend hours visualizing their races or events before performing. They close their eyes and mentally go through every move. Their bodies respond by twitching muscles and firing nerves to match the images in their heads.

- Use visualization to see yourself succeeding at job interviews and in your future work.

- If you are still feeling resentful about being let go, release your negative feelings through this guided visualization. Find a quiet, peaceful place to relax. Now, read:

    Watch and notice as dark, sinister clouds build up in the sky, getting thicker and thicker. Notice that each cloud is filled with a difficult emotion that you felt since your job loss. You see anger, fear, resentment, confusion, shock, disappointment, and worry. They are all there. The dark clouds keep building and building. As they build, the lightning begins to strike, and the rain begins to fall. Watch the storm vent its rage. Then watch as it starts to dissipate. You see the clouds begin to slowly break apart and dissipate, moving in a new direction. Notice the rain has stopped and that the clouds have lightened. Now, see the sun poke its rays out from inside the clouds. Feel the bright, warm sun shed its light on you. Melt as its warmth hugs you and sends light into your soul. Bask in its glory. It is a new day. Darkness has been transformed into light.

CARPE DIEM

What does success on the job look like to you? Visualize it in your mind. See the details of you doing the work and engaging with others.

97.

FEEL EMPOWERED

- To empower literally means to gain a sense of personal power. Empowering is active and uplifting. It stirs positive energy within you. When you are empowered, you feel inspired, motivated, and creative. You feel, well, powerful.

- You can generate a sense of empowerment. Try these ideas:
    - Spend time with people who inspire you.
    - Advocate for yourself. If you feel something isn't right, say so in a calm yet firm manner.
    - Don't allow your emotions to determine how your day unfolds. When you feel painful emotions surface, make a conscious effort to release them. First, acknowledge them by saying something like, "I feel frustrated by XYZ." Then, see them rise and dissipate into the air.
    - Avoid negative people. If someone is ranting or complaining, leave the room. Go outside for a burst of fresh air and re-center yourself.
    - Find a mentor who has lived through job loss and found success.

CARPE DIEM

Make a list of people, activities, and situations that empower you. Pick one and find a way to experience it.

98.

NURTURE YOUR SPIRIT

- As you transcend to a new beginning, you must tend to your spirit. When you nurture your spirit, you take care of the part of yourself that longs for transcendence, the part that is striving to move above and beyond this loss. Your transcendent spirit wants you to surround yourself with compassion and positive self-regard.

- Nuture your spiritual side through:
    - Inspirational readings
    - Moving music
    - Supportive others
    - Prayer or meditation
    - Strolling or meandering
    - Connecting with wise and spiritual people
    - Being in nature
    - Doing things you love

- As you nurture your transcendent spirit, you will find yourself giving attention to your beliefs and values. You'll find yourself turning toward meaning.

CARPE DIEM

Try going beyond your comfort zone and experiment
with a spiritual practice such as prayer, chanting,
or meditation. Try it every day for a week.

99.

GO TO THE WILDERNESS

- You are in liminal space—the gap between what ended and what will be. In liminal space you feel discomfort because it is empty and uncertain.

- As you surrender to the emptiness and uncertainty and stop struggling against it, transformation becomes possible. Transformation is a process. As in nature, there is disintegration before there is reintegration and renewal.

- Historically, during times of transition it was common for an individual to embark on a "passage journey" or "vision quest." During these journeys, the person was intentionally alone and empty in the wilderness. Jesus, Moses, and Buddha all went to the wilderness to discover new visions or gain greater clarity about their futures.

- You are at a crossroads. You are in liminal space. Go to the wilderness. Allow yourself to encounter being alone, quiet, and empty so that you can be filled with the vision of your future.

CARPE DIEM

If you were to take a wilderness journey, where would you go? How long would you be gone? Can you make it happen? Greater clarity about your future awaits.

100.

TRANSFORM YOURSELF

- Transformations often happen during major turning points in your life—times when you are moving from one state of being to another. It is during these transitions that you are given the chance to redefine and rework yourself.

- Transitions provide a break from the wheel of life. You get off and walk around. You look at new scenery. Often, you need this break to see your life for what it really is. Only then can you decide what is working, what's not, and what you want to change, or grow.

- You are experiencing this right now. You are ripe for contemplation. Foster it. Do things that open your mind and shift your perspective. Try something new.

- As the saying goes, "This too shall pass." You will get back on that wheel and start moving again. But you have this chance to pause and think about how the wheel is constructed, what direction it's going, and how fast or slow you want to go. Take this chance. Believe in your future. Transform.

CARPE DIEM

Think of something you would like to change about yourself. Maybe you want to trust yourself more or be a better listener. Make a conscious effort to practice this change for the rest of the week.

A FINAL WORD

Not everything that is faced can be changed easily,
but nothing can be changed unless it is faced.
—James Baldwin

You have come a long way since the day you found out that your job was ending. You faced the shock of it and you weathered the tough emotions that it brought. You grieved and mourned, with the help of others. Finally, you set your intention on what you wanted your career life to look like and you took specific actions to make that intention real. You planted yourself in the ground and became ready to withstand the winds of the day. You grew strong and opened to transformation.

Our hope for you is that you will someday look back on this journey and see that it was a positive and necessary transition in your life—one that pushed you forward to a better place. Our hope is that you find satisfying work that brings you new challenges, new skills, and a profoundly meaningful future.

Remember that the journey through job loss is not always linear. The beginning and ending are not always clear. In grief and mourning, we often need to take steps backward to move forward. If you need to go back and repeat earlier steps, don't judge yourself or worry about your progress. Trust that even when it doesn't feel like it, you are doing the grief work that you need to do.

Spot the horizon. Spot the light at the top of the stairs. Allow this journey to take as long as it needs to take to heal and transform you. Trust the process and keep moving forward with intention.

Remember to take good care of yourself along the way. To be self-nurturing is to have the courage to pay attention to your needs, both at home and with your job search. Above all, self-nurturing is about self-acceptance. Please recognize that it will take both time and willingness to actively participate in mourning. If you commit yourself to authentic mourning, you can and will go on to find meaning and purpose in you life and work.

Every day is a new day and presents a new opportunity to embrace your journey. Each day provides a chance for you to feel your emotions, grieve, mourn, ask for the support of others, get organized, explore what you want, define who you are, and believe in yourself. Make every day count. We have faith in you. We see your future, and it's full of promise.

SEND US YOUR IDEAS
FOR HEALING GRIEF
DURING A JOB LOSS

We'd love to hear your practical ideas for coping after job loss. We may use them in other books someday. Please jot down your idea and mail it to:

Center for Loss and Life Transition
3735 Broken Bow Road
Fort Collins, CO 80526
Or email us at DrWolfelt@centerforloss.com
or go to this website, www.centerforloss.com.

We hope to hear from you!

My idea:

_____

_____

_____

_____

_____

_____

My name and mailing address:

_____

_____

_____

_____

ALSO BY DR. ALAN WOLFELT

Healing Grief at Work

100 Practical Ideas After Your Workplace is Touched by Loss

How should we respond when a colleague dies? What can we do when a coworker's family member dies? What if a tragedy impacts multiple people in the workplace? And if we're grieving, what can we do with our grief 8-5, Monday through Friday?

This book seeks to answer these questions and more in Dr. Wolfelt's practical, compassionate style. Topics covered include effective ways to channel grief during the workday, supporting coworkers who mourn, participating in group memorials, negotiating appropriate bereavement leave, and many others.

Ideas for both the mourner and the mourner's coworkers are included. Purchased in bulk, this book makes an excellent resource for employee in-services as well as general distribution at a time of need.

A special introduction for employers (owners, managers, human resource personnel, EAPs etc.) addresses the economic impact of grief in the workplace (conservatively estimated at $75 billion per year in the US) and provides practical and cost-effective ideas for maintaining morale and creating a productive yet compassionate work environment.

ISBN 978-1-879651-45-6 • 128 pages • softcover • $11.95

Companion
PRESS

All Dr. Wolfelt's publications can be ordered by mail from:
Companion Press
3735 Broken Bow Road
Fort Collins, CO 80526
(970) 226-6050
www.centerforloss.com

ALSO BY DR. ALAN WOLFELT

Healing Your Grieving Soul

100 Spiritual Practices for Mourners

Grief is in large part a spiritual struggle, and turning to spiritual practices in the face of loss helps many people find hope and healing. Following a helpful introduction about the role of spirituality in grief, this practical guide offers tips and activities on meditation, prayer, yoga, solitude and many more. Mourners who are feeling anxious might try breathing exercises. Those experiencing fatigue might try massage. Each idea is accompanied by a "carpe diem," which is a specific activity that the reader can try right that very moment to engage with her grief on the path to healing.

ISBN 978-1-879651-57-9 • 128 pages • softcover • $11.95

Companion
PRESS

All Dr. Wolfelt's publications can be ordered by mail from:
Companion Press
3735 Broken Bow Road
Fort Collins, CO 80526
(970) 226-6050
www.centerforloss.com

ALSO BY DR. ALAN WOLFELT

Healing Your Grieving Body

100 Physical Practices for Mourners
by Alan Wolfelt, Ph.D. and Kirby Duvall, M.D.

Dr. Wolfelt has teamed up with physician Kirby Duvall to pen this practical new guide. Do you have muscle aches and pains, problems with eating and sleeping, low energy, headaches and other physical symptoms since the death of someone loved? When you are grieving, your body often lets you know it feels distressed, too. In fact, you may be shocked by how much your body responds to the impact of your loss. The mind-body connection in grief is profoundly strong, but taking care of your body in the 100 ways described in this new addition to our popular 100 Ideas series will help you soothe your body as you heal your heart and soul.

ISBN 978-1-879651-63-0 • 128 pages • softcover • $11.95

Companion
P R E S S

All Dr. Wolfelt's publications can be ordered by mail from:
Companion Press
3735 Broken Bow Road
Fort Collins, CO 80526
(970) 226-6050
www.centerforloss.com

ALSO BY DR. ALAN WOLFELT

The Mourner's Book of Hope

To integrate loss and to move forward with a life of meaning and love, you must have hope. Hope is a belief in a
good that is yet to be. This beautiful little hardcover gift
book offers Dr. Wolfelt's thoughts on hope in grief inter-
spersed with quotes from the world's greatest hope-filled
thinkers.

ISBN 978-1-879651-65-4 • 200 pages
hardcover • $15.95

Companion
P R E S S

All Dr. Wolfelt's publications can be ordered by mail from:
Companion Press
3735 Broken Bow Road
Fort Collins, CO 80526
(970) 226-6050
www.centerforloss.com

ALSO BY DR. ALAN WOLFELT

Transcending Divorce

Ten Essential Touchstones for Finding Hope and Healing Your Heart

If you're hurting after a divorce, or know someone who is, this book is for you. Warm, direct and easy to understand, this is a book you will not want to put down.

ISBN 978-1-879651-50-0 • 128 pages
softcover • $14.95

Companion
PRESS

All Dr. Wolfelt's publications can be ordered by mail from:
Companion Press
3735 Broken Bow Road
Fort Collins, CO 80526
(970) 226-6050
www.centerforloss.com